TEST
TALK

TEST
TALK

Integrating Test Preparation into Reading Workshop

o o o

Amy H. Greene & Glennon Doyle Melton

o o o

Stenhouse Publishers
Portland, Maine

Stenhouse Publishers
www.stenhouse.com

Credits
Page 50: "When I Am Full of Silence," by Jack Prelutsky. Reprinted with the permission of HarperCollins. Copyright © 1994 by Jack Prelutsky.
Pages 50–51: "Listen," by Nikky Grimes in *It's Raining Laughter*. Reprinted with the permission of Boyds Mills Press, Inc. Copyright © 1997 by Nikky Grimes.
Page 55: "Change," by Effie Lee Newsome. In *The Best Children's Poems of Effie Lee Newsome*, edited by Rudine Bishop. Reprinted with the permission of Boyds Mills Press, Inc. Copyright © 1999 by Rudine Bishop.
Page 75: "Geese," by Effie Lee Newsome. In *The Best Children's Poems of Effie Lee Newsome*, edited by Rudine Bishop. Reprinted with the permission of Boyds Mills Press, Inc. Copyright © 1999 by Rudine Bishop.
Pages 93–94: "I Visualize Myself," by Jane Yang in *Dream Makers: Young People Share Their Hopes and Inspirations*, edited by Neil Waldman. Reprinted with the permission of Boyds Mills Press, Inc. Copyright © 2003 by Neil Waldman.
Pages 108–109: "Grandma," by Ralph Fletcher in *A Writing Kind of Day: Poems for Young Poets*. Reprinted with the permission of Boyds Mills Press, Inc. Copyright © 2005 by Ralph Fletcher.
Pages 110–111: "Poetry Strands," by Ralph Fletcher in *A Writing Kind of Day: Poems for Young Poets*. Reprinted with the permission of Boyds Mills Press, Inc. Copyright © 2005 by Ralph Fletcher.
Page 112: "Losing My Senses," by Sara Holbrook in *Am I Naturally This Crazy?* Reprinted with the permission of Boyds Mills Press, Inc. Copyright © 1996 by Sara Holbrook.

Library of Congress Cataloging-in-Publication Data
Greene, Amy H., 1966—
      Test talk : integrating test preparation into reading workshop / Amy H. Greene and Glennon Doyle Melton ; foreword by Franki Sibberson.
          p. cm.
      Includes bibliographical references.
      ISBN-13: 978-1-57110-461-8 (alk. paper)
      ISBN-10: 1-57110-461-5 (alk. paper)
      1. Test-taking skills--Study and teaching. 2. Reading comprehension. I. Melton, Glennon Doyle, 1976— II. Title.
      LB3060.57.G74 2007
      371.26--dc22   2006100988

Cover and interior design by Catherine Hawkes/Cat & Mouse
Typeset by Cat & Mouse
Cover photograph by Jennifer A. Orr
Chapter photographs by Amy Greene, Michelle Kem, Jennifer Orr, and Tuyen Vu

Manufactured in the United States of America on acid-free paper
13 12 11 10 09 08   9 8 7 6 5 4

Contents

Foreword

Late last September, I was administering our state practice test to my new third graders. Because it was early in the year, and because this was the first test that they would be taking, I thought it was important that they at least see what the test might look like. Even though we were only in the fourth week of school, I wanted to give my students a chance to become familiar with the format of the test so that they would know what to expect.

As teachers, we are used to dealing with tests these days. They are given for many purposes and at many grade levels. We read about them in our professional journals and hear about them as taxpayers of a school district. Many of our parent conferences deal with students' test results. In some districts, test prep seems to have become an academic subject of its own.

Students, too, have heard a lot about state tests. They hear about them on the news and know that they matter. But last September when I administered that practice test, I was surprised at how little my students actually knew about the tests themselves. Instead of filling in bubbles, students were underlining. Students were not always certain as to which questions went with which reading passage. Several students were confused at the term *selection* in the reading portion of the test. Others seemed overwhelmed by the length of the test. It was clear that my students needed some kind of preparation for the standardized test.

If you are like me, you struggle with test preparation. As teachers, most of us don't agree with the testing craze that seems to be trying to take over our classrooms. We know that in many cases, it has become too much for our students and is often doing far more harm than good. The pressure on our students has become overwhelming. I'm resistant because I know that real learning takes time, and we have less time when I have to include test preparation. But I also feel that my students deserve to have the tools to successfully navigate a test. Until big changes occur, the students in our classrooms should be given the opportunity to show their best thinking on the test. We know that these are high-stakes tests for our students, our schools, and our school districts.

When I first read Amy Greene and Glennon Melton's *Test Talk: Integrating Test Preparation into Reading Workshop*, I was thrilled, because it presented ideas for test preparation that would not change good classrooms. This book is a solution to the dilemma most teachers face: how do I prepare my kids for the inevitable tests without sacrificing valuable curriculum? Many test prep programs are on the market for teachers. These programs promise to help prepare our students for the test. But, when we take just a few seconds to flip through many of them, it is clear that implementing these programs is not at all the way we want to spend our time with students. We can't help but wonder how much instructional time is lost in the name of testing when we use these prepackaged programs. I know teachers who have used test preparation programs beginning on the first day of school. We only have six to seven hours each day with our students. Do we really want to have them spending part of each day doing mindless test preparation work that mimics the test in that they don't actually learn anything? Of course not.

Test Talk shows teachers how they can run great reading and writing workshops and still prepare students for tests in a thoughtful way that is respectful of their needs. Amy Greene and Glennon Melton are teachers who are going through what all of us are—the struggle to make sure our students are prepared for tests without sacrificing learning. They have figured out a way to maintain the integrity of their classrooms while preparing students to do well on the required standardized tests.

In the classrooms in this book, teachers run effective reading workshops. Students are engaged in daily reading and writing. They are discovering new ideas and growing as readers. They are talking to one another about books. They are learning to comprehend text. The authors have built on the success of their reading workshops to help kids make sense of tests as a genre. Amy and Glennon remind us that we, the teachers, are the decision-makers in our classrooms. They designed a plan that works for their students by supporting them as both learners and as test takers. What struck me most as I read *Test Talk* was the strategic way in which students approached test questions. The authors describe three beliefs that hold true throughout the book: (1) successful test takers first have to be smart readers; (2) successful test takers need to be able to translate the unique language of the test; and (3) learning how to be a successful test taker can be fun. The lessons invite students to look for clues in the test directions, to examine characteristics of the test such as the question formats, to become familiar with "test talk" vocabulary, and to look for phrasing such as the poetry terms *stanza* and *line*.

Clearly, Amy and Glennon understand the nature of learning. Helping their students make sense of the test in this way was brilliant! I can't wait to use their ideas in my own classroom. These students made great discoveries that would help them take tests because they were in a true workshop classroom.

Test Talk provides an answer for teachers who want an approach that is truly valuable for their students. It is clear that Amy, Glennon, and the teachers at their school worked hard to make the best of a very difficult situation—and succeeded.

Franki Sibberson

Acknowledgments

We get by with a little help from our friends.

We would like to thank the following friends and colleagues for inspiring our teaching, supporting our writing, and making our lives richer:

Andrew Ajemian, Beth Aldonas, Pat Altenburger, Lisa Antonelli, Barbara Anzalone, Judy Bailey, Mary Barker, Jennifer Baskette, Jenny Braun, Karen Brunn, Susan Call, Julie Colella, Michele Dusek, Andrea Garris, Julie Greene, Cathy Hurley, Michelle Jones, Jennifer Kalletta, Michelle Kem, Wendy McColley, Kelly McCullers, Ann Monday, Charlene O'Brien, Jennifer Orr, Tuyen Vu, Suzanne Whaley, Catherine Weiss, Phylis Williams, and Tina Yalen.

Special thanks to Mary Ann Ryan for creating the vision and to Chris Dickens for seeing it through, and to both of them for believing in us.

Thank you to Bill Varner, our editor, for believing that we had something important to say, and for guiding us and making us laugh while we figured out how to say it.

And finally, to the staff and children of Annandale Terrace: you are the embodiment of a learning community, and we are so proud to be part of that.

Amy Greene and Glennon Melton

I am especially grateful to my friend and mentor, Noel Ridge. You nudged me when I needed it and taught me that there is no limit to what children can learn. To Stephanie Bisson, Pat Fege, Jean Frey, Larry Kugler, Carleen Payne, Stephanie Phillips, and Mary Schulman, thanks for your unending support and guidance from the early days and beyond. I also want to thank Heather Speicher and Kevin Duffy, for sharing their wisdom and words, and Kathleen Fay, for my first writing conferences and for just listening. Finally, I want to thank my friend Glennon, a special spirit, wise writer, and someone who teaches while she learns.

Amy

Thank you to my husband, Craig, for walking beside me and holding my hand on this and every other journey—and for turning every dream of mine into a dream of ours. Thank you to my dad, Dick, for teaching me how to write and how to live. To my mom, Patti, thank you for being my inspiration as a wife, mother, sister, and teacher. To Sister, Amanda, thank you for always being my strength, and for letting me be yours. To my babies, Chase and Tish, thank you for making my heart explode ten times a day. To Michelle Banning, Adrianne Brubaker, Andria Eppes, Juliet Finnegan, and Sharisa Lewis, thank you for teaching me that you can get through anything with the love of God and good friends. Lastly, thank you to Amy, my mentor and friend. Your talent, wisdom, and dedication to children are the backbone of this book.

Glennon

1 | Beyond Hope and Honeybuns: Changing Our Approach to Test Preparation

"Hope is not a Strategy." After a long day of teaching, this phrase, in bold letters on a projection screen, greeted our exhausted staff as we entered the first staff meeting of the school year. Concerned and anxious whispers filled the library of Annandale Terrace Elementary School. We knew our Virginia Standards of Learning (SOL) scores were in, and we judged by the faces of our administrators that they were not good. Our principal announced that our scores were well below what was expected, especially in third grade, where many students were just learning to read in English. This year, the stakes were high. According to the federal No Child Left Behind Act, we were at risk of not making "adequate yearly progress." Not making AYP meant that local parents could send their children to other schools. This prospect was devastating to a staff so passionate about our students and our community.

In addition to our passion for our students, we also considered ourselves a progressive staff. However, many of us would have been quick to admit that there was nothing cutting-edge about our approach to preparing our students for standardized tests. Frankly, much of our staff didn't believe that standardized tests had any relevance to our students' needs. We shared a general consensus that these tests evaluate only certain kinds of intelligence and that many bright, talented students were not able to demonstrate their strengths on the tests. Because most of our children come from low income families and/or had recently arrived from another country, they had not had the benefit of starting school at an early age. Students in more affluent communities, including the children of the politicians demanding the test, probably began their educations years before our kids set foot in a classroom. For this and other reasons, most of our immigrant children and children of poverty also lacked the command of the language that the test demands.

We knew that the existing standardized reading tests were not the most effective tools for assessing readers or evaluating schools. Along with many educators across the country, we believed that when teachers spent time preparing students to read short texts and answer multiple-choice questions, they were not preparing students to be strong readers. Our staff prefers using authentic assessment such as running records, andecdotal records, the Developmental Reading Assessment, and

Concepts about Print to drive our teaching. We also believed the SOL tests were specifically biased against nonnative English speakers. Through informal assessment, we had demonstrated repeatedly that our students knew the test content. Because we lacked faith in our state SOL test as a true assessment of our students' progress, we minimized its importance. We taught our hearts out from the moment each student entered our school. Then, when SOL week arrived, we stopped teaching and told our students to get a good night's sleep and to do their best. On the morning of the test, we gave them honeybuns for breakfast and crossed our fingers. The students were confused and stressed, and so were we, but we told them that soon it would all be over and we could go back to real life. Then No Child Left Behind came about and the SOL test took on a new significance. Our students would have to pass this test in order for us to continue serving them, and they would also need to pass to graduate from high school and move toward college and productive professional lives.

The Annandale Terrace staff is a community of learners. We expect rigorous discourse about students and their learning. We learn from one another, as well as from outside resources. We share, research, advise, collaborate, coach, question, and listen. We are a team. We are a progressive, broad-minded staff, and our administrators hire people who are a match. Our staff researches and analyzes new instructional techniques across the curriculum; we don't adopt every new technique to which we are exposed. Because of this community of care, trust, and professionalism, morale is high. But the day that we learned about our poor test scores and the subsequent threat to our school, we felt demoralized. We ultimately responded to the challenge of low test scores in a way that boosted our scores and morale. This book describes our response and new approach, but first, here is a glimpse into our Annandale Terrace, a school community worth saving.

Portrait of Our School

We are passionate about our school. The students of Annandale Terrace are inspiring new Americans who come from forty-four countries and speak thirty-five languages. Our students' parents came to this country to give their children a better education and a better life. Many have sacrificed everything for this dream, and they trust us to help fulfill it. The power of this responsibility and privilege resonates through our classrooms and hallways. The entire staff is dedicated to preparing our students academically and socially for the world in which they will become adults. We have high expectations for one another, and no one is afraid of hard work.

The Annandale Terrace staff believes that our students' education must reach far beyond the curriculum. Like teachers everywhere, we are dedicated to including the whole family in the educational experience, and to reaching out to the communities from which our students come. Annandale Terrace is located in a part of Fairfax County, Virginia, where gang activity is at an all-time high. Many of our students share apartment buildings or even homes with gang members. Most students don't speak English at home; they have adult responsibilities like translating for their parents. We know that providing our students and parents the special skills needed to meet these challenges is crucial. Based on the percentage of children who receive free and reduced lunch, we are designated a Title I school by the federal government. In the past we used these funds to target and serve groups of high-needs students, but years ago we shifted to the schoolwide model, which means that the money helps provide a better education for all our students. Our staff and administration use the grant money in different ways each year, but some of our constants are resource teachers, parent liaisons, instructional materials, and staff developers in math and language arts.

As a staff, we have realized several important points about our professional development. First, it is critical to stick with an instructional focus for more than a year. For the last five years, we have worked with the same language arts staff developer. We have also adopted the Literacy Collaborative model, both primary and intermediate. This reform model includes a consistent instructional framework, frequent coaching sessions, and bimonthly after-school coursework. Through these staff development models, we have built common beliefs, understandings, and expectations across grade levels. Students no longer need to reinvent themselves as readers and writers to meet different teachers' criteria. We found that after one year, we had only just begun to improve our instruction.

Keeping the majority of our staff development in-house has proved invaluable. Sending a few teachers out to see "experts" can't compare to participating together in ongoing, relevant, needs-based staff development that builds on previous learning. The one-shot workshop no longer holds the same credibility for us. *We know that real change and success take time.*

In order to further meet the challenges our students face, we have modified our school calendar so that students attend school year round. This calendar provides the usual 184 instructional days but swaps the long summer break for shorter breaks every nine weeks. This provides for a safe, consistent environment in which students are immersed in learning and the English language without extended interruptions. During the short vacations, we offer intersession classes, which are designed to be a mixture of summer school and summer camp. Classes like cooking, tennis, and media arts are designed to broaden a student's life experiences as well as address academics. Intersession classes offer our students special extracurricular activities that may not have been available to them through other means.

Our school has a parent center where parents, relatives, and guardians are invited to inquire about the school and their children's classes, have coffee, visit, and volunteer. Parents also have the opportunity to learn computer and job skills and to seek support with the challenges that accompany a transition into a new culture. Our parent center is run by three parent liaisons and one parent resource teacher who offer weekly Parent Coffees to address issues that range from dealing with gang violence to helping a struggling reader at home. Our parent liaisons also coordinate our families' needs for translators. Translators in several languages are available for every parent conference and evening program, and all paperwork that is sent home is translated into several languages. Our students' parents are eager to be a part of the school and to learn about their children's educational experiences, and this commitment to translations bridges the language divide between us. Our staff is as dedicated to learning from our students' parents as they are to learning from us. Every year we hold a parent panel at a staff meeting. We ask parents from different countries to discuss their cultures and share information that may give teachers a better understanding of the students' backgrounds. Each year these parents and many others thank the teachers by hosting a Valentine's dinner, at which the international spread is matched only by the entertainment. Students come dressed in their cultural garb and perform songs and dances from their countries.

The Annandale Terrace guidance counselors work overtime to meet the community's needs. During the holidays, they and the parent liaisons organize a giving tree for our neediest families. Parents sign up and offer gift suggestions for their children, and our staff shops for the gifts. This is just one of the ways we emphasize our commitment to one another all year long.

We have many reasons to be confident that our school provides a supportive and rigorous environment for our students to learn. When we heard the low test scores in the staff meeting that we described at the beginning of this chapter, the numbers stood in stark contrast to what we knew we accomplished every day.

Hope Is Not a Strategy

We never doubted the potential of our students; we knew our problems lay elsewhere. After the meeting that revealed our disappointing test scores, many of us decided it was time to stop minimizing and complaining and start exploring the huge disconnect between our students' actual abilities and what they showed on the test. We asked ourselves two new questions: (1) Why do our students need to pass standardized tests? and (2) How can we help our students show what they know on standardized tests?

The first question was easily answered. We admitted that it was not just because of state and federal pressures. Test taking is a life skill. We wanted our kids to have every advantage, and we agreed that successful test takers have an advantage. While we still asserted that the SOL test was flawed, we concluded that it was only the first of many biased tests our students would face throughout their lives. In fact, much of their academic and professional success throughout life would be based upon their performance on tests. They would face these state tests throughout high school, take the SAT to get into college, and then take more standardized tests to enter graduate school. Many would need to pass standardized tests to further their careers; professions from restaurant employee to CPA to teacher require success on tests just to get a foot in the door. Our ideal educational and professional worlds, we agreed, would have no standardized tests. But a perfect world would not contain "stranger danger" either, yet we would never dream of neglecting this issue in school and sending our kids into the world unprepared. We decided it was our duty as educators to prepare our students for the challenges of the real world, not a perfect one. We decided that we would do whatever it took to help our students beat this test—except give up powerful, purposeful instruction. We would create a concrete, purposeful test-taking curriculum, and we would integrate it before a less meaningful test preparation program was imposed upon us. We embarked on the work of addressing the second question, How can we help our students show what they know on standardized tests?

Our first meeting of the year became the catalyst for a paradigm shift in the minds of many members our staff. This new way of thinking continues to evolve today. After patching our wounded egos, we fell back on our mantra that we are learners as well as teachers, and we began to revamp and even reverse some of our thinking. Soon after the meeting in the library, interested staff members began to meet informally to plan more thoughtful test-taking preparation. We chose to focus on reading because our kids needed to pass this test for NCLB, and because they were struggling with this test more than with math. We studied released items from our SOL reading test. We took this material home, read and reread, and looked for patterns and problems. We took the test as if we were students and tried to imagine what they would be thinking as they studied each passage and possible answer. Early in our research, we discovered a few truths.

First, the reading test was hard—not necessarily because of the content being tested, but because of the language and format the test writers used. The test was written in English, but not the same English that our kids spoke or even the same English that we used to teach them. The language was very formal, the kind that *A Teacher's Guide to Standardized Reading Tests: Knowledge Is Power* (Calkins et al. 1998) refers to as *hyper-English*. We also discovered very clear patterns in the reading tests. Although the same basic skills were tested repeatedly, the language changed each time. For example, the tests contained several questions about finding the main idea, but each question used different vocabulary; most didn't even use the term *main idea*. One question asked students to finish the sentence, "This passage is mainly about...," and another asked for "the best summary of the passage." We knew our kids could find the main idea while reading; they had been learning this concept since kindergarten. But they couldn't tell which questions on the test were actually asking them to find the main idea, because the language the test used was foreign to them! In other words, we didn't have to ask ourselves, "Are we teaching main idea?" We just had to ask, "How can we help kids identify and answer main idea questions on the test?"

The Genesis of Test Talk

As more and more of our focus shifted to the language used on the test, we realized that language was a strong emphasis in other areas of our instruction. Why not in test taking? Translating a foreign language to a familiar one was a skill that many of our students had practiced in their daily lives for years, but we weren't teaching them how to use this skill to succeed on standardized tests. We taught kids many specific systems of language—for math, science, social studies, daily English language, even manners and etiquette—that were subject- and audience-specific. We needed to do the same for test taking: to teach our students the specific language needed to decode the test. We decided to call this language *test talk*.

Second, we agreed that the formats used in reading tests were confusing our students. Most of them had probably never before seen a passage or poem with phrases underlined and lines numbered, nor were they accustomed to dealing with multiple choices or reading small fonts. As adult test takers, we make test formats more understandable by using strategies like underlining important information and rereading confusing sentences. Our students knew how to use some of these strategies as readers of other genres, but not necessarily as test takers. If they were to succeed, applying reading strategies to tests would need to become second nature to them.

Finally, we discussed how long and laborious these tests must be for children. Never in the classroom setting would we ask children to sit, read unfamiliar material, and answer questions for hours and hours at a time. Successful marathon runners don't show up on race day untrained, but we were asking our kids to arrive on test day and face the test without the stamina that they needed.

As a group, we decided that our research had led us to good news and bad news. The good news was that our problem was not content related; our kids knew this stuff. There was more good news: we were very confident in our reading and writing workshops and the results they produced. The bad news was that our approach to teaching kids how to take a test differed greatly from the rest of our thoughtful teaching. When teaching any other new concept, we connected the new skill to the known, gave our kids concrete examples, modeled, and gradually released responsibility. After observation and informal assessment, we retaught in small groups or individually, based on need.

In contrast, we had never taught our kids how to take a test. We only asked them to practice, practice, practice. It was like introducing division by asking students to do sixty problems without ever showing them how to divide. We know as educators that *practice is not preparation*; skills must be taught in a concrete, meaningful way before they can be practiced. This is even more critical with standardized tests because they are written in a language that is challenging for most students. When our students opened that thick booklet on test day, it was the first time many of them had seen the language and format, and it was certainly the first time they had ever been asked to concentrate on such difficult material, without a break, for so long. We realized that this was setting them up for failure. In order to be successful on these tests, our kids needed several new skills. They had to be able to translate the test writers' formal English (test talk) into kid talk, recognize and categorize questions into concepts they had been taught in class, understand and successfully manipulate the format of the test, and use test-taking strategies to be proactive test takers. They also needed the stamina to sustain their concentration through the test.

From Resolve to Action

At this point we began developing lessons to teach our kids the testing skills they needed and integrating them during the school year. We also knew that by the end of the year, when the test came, our kids needed many reading concepts reviewed. In every other subject, we used games and engaging activities for review, but in reading we had no review plan. So we identified the major concepts in the standardized tests and created concrete, exciting, and meaningful review lessons to address each one. We also organized the language that the test used and created test talk lessons that would help our kids begin to decode the test. We researched the test-taking strategies they would need and created lessons to teach these strategies and opportunities to practice them. Finally, we developed a plan to help our kids start developing the stamina they would need on test day, mainly by continuing to encourage long blocks of independent reading time with varied genres.

As many teachers began integrating these lessons and ideas into their classrooms, our staff and students started speaking the same test-taking language, just as we shared language for reading and writing instruction. We believe that these lessons and our new overall approach to the test were the reasons that our scores rose significantly the following year and our school was taken off probation.

The next two years continued to present us with challenges. After three years of climbing scores, one grade level's scores fell dramatically. The drop frustrated and confused the staff members who had worked so hard and had experienced so much success during the last few years. After much thought (and no sudden moves), we remembered the biggest lessons from our testing and language arts work and research: education is not an exact science. *Real change and success take time.* We decided to refocus our energy and continue to believe in our staff and our students.

We believe that a major key to long-term success is positive and level-headed reaction to test scores from teachers and administrators. Of course, every staff member's tolerance for change is different, but this basic levelheadedness must be grounded in a staff's common beliefs about how kids learn, and in unwillingness to waver from best practice. A staff must be committed first to powerful, purposeful reading instruction. In our school, where teachers were team teaching successfully in writing and reading workshops, we had developed a common and consistent teaching language across the building. Because our instructional decisions were assessment driven, we were making stronger instructional decisions and becoming more knowledgeable and confident every year. So when we tackled the testing problem, the instruction piece was already in place. We understood that reading workshop, including daily whole-group, small-group, and one-on-one instruction, wouldn't change. It would not be put on the chopping block. We weren't going to stop teaching our kids to be broad, strategic readers. We weren't going to give up read-alouds. No one said, "Let's cut out independent reading time." These were all nonnegotiable. We knew we needed to integrate test-taking skills into our reading workshop without letting them take over our curriculum or routines. We wouldn't abandon strong instruction for an hour of test-taking practice a day, because we considered our students life-long learners and readers, not just test scores.

Three Fundamental Beliefs About Preparing Students for Testing

As teachers, many of us feel uneasy when we stop reading instruction to implement a traditional test-prep program. It feels unnatural to put meaningful reading teaching aside and ask students to read passages and answer sample questions, which is what most test-prep programs require us to do. We feel guilty when we do this, because we see how frustrating and boring this type of program is to our students. We are conflicted because we know that we need to prepare our students for the reading test, but we also know there must be a better way. There is a better way—an authentic and meaningful way to prepare students for standardized reading tests, and it's based upon the following three fundamental beliefs:

1. Successful test takers must first be smart readers.

It is not enough for students to know the content of the test; they must also be flexible and strategic readers. When students approach the test, they need to know that *standardized reading tests are a genre*, not a mystery, and that they can succeed if they apply general and genre-specific reading strategies. Many test-taking strategies are simply good reading strategies, so students should be taught to attack a test just as they would any other genre. *Test-taking instruction that is meaningful and effective for students should be integrated into reading workshop*, not just isolated as a review unit. Test taking has long been "hidden curriculum," but now we need to give it the attention it demands.

2. Successful test takers must be able to translate the unique language of the test.

Standardized reading tests use formal language that is completely foreign to many students. We teach students specific language for every other subject because we know that they need a command of the language in order to truly understand the content. For example, science teachers know that if they ask a student to read directions for and perform a science experiment without teaching that *hypothesis* is "science talk" for *educated guess*, the student won't get past the first direction. We need to apply the same premise to teaching test taking. When a student reads a test question that says, "The author of this passage included paragraph three in order to…," he or she needs to know that *passage* means *text*, and that *included … in order to* is just test talk for asking about author's intent. Students are helpless on standardized reading tests if they can't decipher test talk.

3. Learning to be a successful test taker can be fun!

Drudgery. Boring. Excruciating. These are a few words our colleagues used to describe traditional test-preparation programs. It's hard to teach material that bores us to tears, so imagine how hard it is to try to *learn* that way. We know that children learn best when they are actively engaged, and we work hard to make their experiences in math, reading, science, and social studies as concrete and exciting as possible. We know that there are visual, auditory, and kinesthetic learners in our classrooms, so we ensure that our students are thinking, discussing, moving, and laughing during our lessons. But when it comes to teaching test taking, too many of us abandon everything we know about children as learners and ask students to sit silently at their desks while they read passage after passage and answer question after question. What happened to inquiry? What happened to dialogue? What happened to fun?

By now you're probably asking the same question we did: How and when does a teacher with a daily one-hour reading block and a class full of diverse readers apply these principles about test-taking instruction during his or her already jam-packed school day? For us, the vehicle is carefully planned units of study taught during daily reading workshops. These units simplify test taking by connecting it to our students' other reading.

Teaching Within the Reading Workshop

A unit is an in-depth study of a strategy or skill that will help students become stronger readers and thinkers. Successfully applying a new skill requires time to think, process, discuss, and practice it with the support of an expert. As teachers, we can certainly relate to this concept. We attend so many staff development workshops at which a well-meaning expert throws a *ton* of great information at us and then, while our heads are still spinning says, "Well, my time us up. Good luck!" The topic is never revisited and we don't have time to discuss the meaning of it all with our colleagues, but we are expected to integrate the new skill into our classrooms. Needless to say, we feel defeated and frustrated after these workshops. That's exactly how our students feel when we expect them to apply a new skill after just one lesson. A unit of study eliminates the "one-shot" problem, because the teacher introduces and models application of a new skill over an extended period of time, gradually releasing responsibility throughout the unit until students are able to use the skill independently.

We teach these units of study during the reading workshop. Like the family dinner table, reading workshop provides a comfortable and predictable structure for growing and reflecting, giving students the opportunity to learn from their teacher and peers. The workshop begins with a mini-lesson, followed by independent reading and conferences, reading groups and/or literature discussions, and share time. The focus of the mini-lesson is often carried into each component of the workshop, so that the focus resonates throughout the hour. The mini-lesson allows for whole-group instruction as students gather close to the teacher while he or she models application of the focus skill, often through techniques like shared reading and reading aloud.

Next, students practice the focus skill and enjoy their "just-right books," or books that match their reading level, during independent reading time, while the teacher meets with students for one-on-one reading conferences. This reading conference is an opportunity for personal connection, something that teachers and students crave during a busy school day. It's a conversation during which two readers discuss their thoughts, habits, and challenges. In *How's It Going: A Practical Guide to Conferring with Student Writers* (2000), Carl Anderson says, "The writing conference is not the icing on the cake, it IS the cake" (3). We feel the same about reading conferences. After conferences, small-group instruction provides the students a safe, structured forum to practice the focus skill (or other needed skill) and learn from one another, with support from the teacher. During group time, the other students may be involved in meaningful literacy centers or extended independent reading. Finally, the workshop ends the way it began, with the students gathering to share their successes and challenges as readers.

The decision about what units of study to teach during reading workshop is one of the most important choices a reading teacher makes. Unit ideas should be generated not only from district and state standards, but also from the teacher's beliefs about what strong readers need. Just as we hope you will, we used our professional literature, past standardized tests, colleagues' expertise, and our own experience as readers to identify four critical and universal reading workshop units to focus on in this book: (1) understanding main idea, (2) author's intent, (3) inferring, and (4) poetry. We have also included a chapter on word study, a subject commonly included on standardized tests. We know that your beliefs and state standards may differ from ours, and we hope that these unit ideas will motivate you to customize your reading workshop according to your class's needs.

Navigating the Chapters of This Book

In order to be effective test takers, students must first be effective readers. Many test-prep programs ask teachers to stop authentic, meaningful instruction to teach gimmicks and mnemonic devices related only to testing strategies. This practice supports the idea that the test is unrelated to other learning and gives students another list of meaningless jargon to recall on the day of the test. In order to simplify test taking for students, we need to relate it to their other reading throughout the year by teaching them that a test is simply a genre to which general and specific reading strategies must be applied.

A master carpenter brings the same toolbox to every job and skillfully chooses the proper tools for individual tasks. Similarly, a master reader approaches every text with a collection of general skills and strategies and knows when to apply the ones that are specific to a particular genre. For example, students should know that activating schema, rereading, and using authors' clues are general reading strategies that they should apply to all genres, including the test. Students also need an arsenal of genre-specific strategies, such as looking for clues in a mystery or eliminating test answers that don't match. Chapter 2 consists of lessons that teach both general and test-specific strategies. These lessons should not be taught in isolation, but throughout the year within related units of study.

Each subsequent chapter focuses on a particular reading content skill that often appears on standardized reading tests. Each chapter begins with an introduction, followed by narratives of classroom lessons that show how different teachers weave testing as a skill into workshops in a meaningful way. These narratives are composites that combine many different lessons we've observed and taught and experiences we've had with children. The first narrative features lessons during units of study related to the chapter's focus skill. The second narrative models how to end each unit of study with a test talk lesson, demonstrating how to teach students to relate their real learning in the unit to a standardized test. Both narratives show how authentic and powerful test-taking lessons can be when they are fully integrated.

After the narratives, we have provided a series of lesson plans that can be combined and used as a review in the weeks prior to the test. Again, it is crucial that this review unit come after students have learned these skills throughout the year during meaningful units of study. Each series includes three types of lessons. The first, a Concept Review Plan, gets the students excited and activates their background knowledge of a previously studied concept by reintroducing the concept in a fun and innovative way. The second, a Test Talk Lesson, reviews the related test talk and its meaning. In the third lesson, Practice with Texts, students practice synthesizing their content, test talk, and strategy knowledge. They work on practice passages and questions that attempt to recreate the test situation as closely as possible so that the students can put all their learning "to the test." Each of these lessons starts with a Target Question that serves to foster the kids' ownership of their learning. Each lesson's Target Question indicates a skill that will "make the test easier," building students' test-taking confidence.

We hope that this book will make test-taking instruction practical for you, meaningful for your students, and illustrate that it is possible to improve test scores while honoring your principles as a teacher.

More Than Meets the Eye: Developing Strategies That Help Readers Become Test Takers

I had the flour, eggs, oil, and measuring cups—everything the recipe said I needed to make the "easy chocolate chip birthday cake" that my two-year-old son wanted. Everything, that is, except a sifter. The recipe said I'd need it, but I didn't have a sifter, or even know what one was. I figured my flour would be all right unsifted. How important could that part be? To say that I was far from a gourmet baker would be an understatement. Actually, this was my first cake attempt, but a friend had made it before and assured me it was simple. Besides, I knew how to read and follow directions. Isn't that all that baking requires?

After collecting my materials, I started reading the recipe. I didn't get far. The third step said, "Fold the chocolate chips into the dough." Huh? What did *fold* mean? I checked the back of the cookbook for a glossary. Nothing. I called my sister, an expert baker, for help. Not home. I decided all I could do was guess that *fold* meant *mix*, and carried on. The next steps proved just as confusing, so I guessed and got more and more frustrated.

Finally, I put the cake in the oven and crossed my fingers. After an hour of stress, I opened the oven and found ... a mess. The cake was cracked and flat, and when I tried to flip it onto a plate, it completely fell apart. I had forgotten to grease the pan, and I hadn't known to leave the cake in the pan until it cooled. I sat down, cursed the cookbook author and my friend who gave me the recipe, and felt defeated. Later I discussed the tragedy with my sister, the baker. We agreed that bakers speak a common language. Through experience, they develop a repertoire of kitchen skills and strategies that make certain tasks, impossible for a novice, second nature to a baker. We concluded that there was more to baking than following directions. I decided to head to the grocery store for some good old store-bought cupcakes, because baking required many more skills than were apparent at first glance.

Students required to take a test can feel as frustrated and defeated as I did that day in the kitchen if they don't have the vocabulary, background experience, or strategies necessary for success. Like a recipe, every question on a standardized test evaluates more knowledge than first meets the eye.

At Annandale Terrace, recognizing this reality was the first step toward changing the way we think about test preparation. Each question on a test, we realized, asks students to employ multiple strategies. For example, according to published test material, the following question evaluates a student's ability to identify the main idea. As you read this question, consider all of the reading strategies a student would need in order to answer correctly.

Use the following poem to answer question 7.

Peaceful Place

1 Waves roll
2 Gulls fly
3 Children splash
4 Adults lounge
5 Sun shines
6 Breeze Blows
7 Sand crunches
8 Peaceful Place

7. This poem is mainly about

    A ocean animals.
    B relaxing at the beach.
    C building sandcastles.
    D the sea.

The question looks simple at first, and certainly it does ask students to identify the main idea. But the question also evaluates the following *general* reading strategies:

- Actively reading at this level
- Inferring
- Visualizing
- Activating schema
- Rereading
- Using context clues to understand new and challenging vocabulary
- Using author's clues
- Exercising stamina

In addition, the question evaluates these *genre-specific* strategies:

- Understanding poetry conventions
- Navigating test format
- Following and understanding written directions
- Eliminating answers that don't match
- Translating "test talk"

Broken down this way, what's required from our poor students on every test question looks overwhelming. In fact, the fewer years a student has been attending school and/or learning English, the more skills test taking requires. Luckily, this process can become natural for students if they learn to approach the test as they would any other specific genre: ready to access a repertoire of general and genre-specific reading strategies.

This chapter consists of two types of strategy lessons that can be easily implemented into your reading workshop throughout the year. The general reading strategy lessons, which show students how to apply previously learned reading strategies to the test, can be integrated into reading strategies units. For example, the Rereading Strategies Saves the Day lesson could be taught at the end of a unit about the importance of rereading across all genres. The test-specific strategies should initially be taught within a unit of study about standardized tests as a genre. Both types of lessons can be combined and adapted to create a review unit of all strategies that are especially helpful to test takers in your state. We hope that these lessons will be generative as you adjust them to fit your own test and the needs of your particular students.

• • • GENERAL READING STRATEGY LESSONS

STRATEGY

Reading actively

Reading is thinking. In order to comprehend, strong readers may predict, make connections, ask questions, infer, visualize, determine what is most important, notice themes, critique, evaluate, synthesize, or do myriad other types of thinking while they read. Readers must think while they are reading words to be successful on a standardized test. This lesson should not be the first time different types of thinking such as asking questions and visualizing are introduced. To learn to use these strategies, students need opportunities to practice them individually during long units of study.

Target Question:
Do I know how thinking while I read will make the test easier?

Materials:
- Practice test passage on transparency
- Just-right texts (texts that match the students' reading levels)
- Hard copies of practice test passages

Demonstration:
Write a long-division problem on the board. Think aloud while solving the problem. Make sure to model the different kinds of thinking you're doing—dividing, adding, subtracting. Explain to students that if you didn't do different kinds of thinking when you attempt to solve a division problem, you wouldn't fully understand the problem or get the answer correct.

Connect this idea to reading. If you don't think while you read, you won't understand the text, including standardized test passages.

Put your chosen text on the overhead and read it to the students. Explain that good test takers do many kinds of thinking while reading test passages so they can understand and then answer questions about the passages.

Think aloud while you read the text. Model active reading strategies like connecting, inferring, visualizing, and synthesizing. Record your thinking by writing in the margins as you think aloud. For example, you may record a prediction and then explain how this helps you as a reader. After you finish reading and modeling your thinking, begin to answer the practice questions. Instead of simply answering each one, show how your thinking during reading helps you develop the answers. Draw arrows from the correct answer to thinking that supports that answer in the margin.

Student Practice:

Give each pair of students a practice test passage that includes questions and answer choices. Ask them to read the passage and record their thinking in the margins. They should answer each question and be prepared to connect their answer to their thinking.

Share:

Each pair of students should share a few examples of the thinking they did when they read their passage. Then they should share one question and be prepared to support their answer with thinking done while reading. Record this strategy on your Test-Taking Strategies anchor chart.

Assess:

Notice students who need further intervention. Passive readers will need similar follow-up lessons in small group.

• • •

STRATEGY

Activating schema

A person's schema, or background knowledge, is everything that she has stored in her brain from her past learning and experiences. Activating schema before reading is a crucial and highly effective strategy for readers and test takers. It requires the reader to predict the format and content of a text and to ask herself what she already knows about the subject before she begins reading. This strategy prepares the reader to tackle a challenging text.

Target Question:

Do I know how activating my schema will make the test easier?

Materials:

- Summer gear (visor, sunglasses, beach ball, etc.)
- Posterboard
- Overheads of sample test passages or poems
- Practice test passages and poems for partner work

Demonstration:

Start the lesson by telling the students that you are very excited because you are taking a vacation to Antarctica. Explain that you bought a new outfit to wear when you arrive there and ask them if they'd like to see it. Step into the hallway and put on your summer gear. When you come back in, ask the kids to share out what might be wrong with your outfit. When they tell you that your clothing is not appropriate for freezing weather, explain that you didn't know it was cold in Antarctica, and that you must not have done the necessary research, thinking, and preparing that a vacation requires. Ask them what would have happened to your vacation if you had arrived unprepared for the weather. Discuss possibilities.

Write this question on the board: "What is something you do regularly that you have to prepare for first?" Allow time for partners to discuss. Possible responses may be going to school, going to bed, vacationing, exercising, etc. Ask students what the outcome of these daily events might be if they did not prepare for them. Would they be as successful? Explain that good readers prepare for their reading in a similar way. Just as runners stretch their muscles before a race, readers stretch their brains before reading. If a reader begins a difficult book, passage, or poem without preparing his brain, he will not be as successful or understand the text as well as he would have if he had prepared.

Explain to students that when they begin a new book, passage, or poem, they should *activate their schema* to prepare. This means that they should think about what they already know about the subject by asking this question suggested by testing consultant Dan Mulligan, "Hey, brain, what do I know about...?" Write this question on a poster beneath the title Activating Your Schema.

Tell the students that good test takers also use this skill. When they come to a new passage or poem, they read the title, look at pictures or other clues, and ask their brain what it already knows about the subject. Lead a think-aloud with a sample passage to demonstrate this process. Then practice with different samples as a class.

Student Practice:
Pass out copies of practice test passages and ask the students to practice activating their schema with partners. Remind them to look at the title and ask, "Hey, brain, what do I know about...?" If they don't know the meaning of a word or how to read part of a title, advise them to look at

chunks they do know and activate their schema about those smaller words. Have them write down everything that was in their schema about the title subject. Remind students that since everyone has different experiences, everyone's schema is different. Circulate and make sure students are practicing this strategy accurately.

Share:

Allow students to share out about their experiences activating their schema with their partners. What was easy? What was hard? Is this strategy helpful? Why or why not?

In closing, write this question on the board: "*Why* do good readers and test takers activate their schema before they read?" Discuss. Then change the question to "*How* do readers and test takers activate their schema before they read?" Discuss.

Remind students to use this strategy during independent reading time, and encourage them to tell you anytime throughout the day that they activate their schema. Record this strategy on your Test-Taking Strategies anchor chart.

Assess:

During practice and share time, notice which students need further intervention. Meet with these students in small groups for more practice. Revisit this strategy often and remind students to use it during all of their reading.

• • •

STRATEGY
Using the author's clues to recognize important information

Authors of tests, just like authors of other genres, use textual clues as a signal to readers about which text is important. Students can get lost in the sheer volume of the text on standardized reading tests unless they're able to find and use clues such as bold, underlined, boxed, or italicized text. The ability to use author's clues to isolate crucial text helps readers of all genres.

Target Question:

Do I know how to find and use the test authors' clues to make the test easier?

Materials:
- Mystery text
- Copies of sample test pages
- Copies of chart

Demonstration:

Write these questions on the board: What is a clue? Who uses clues? Give the students time to discuss the questions. After sharing out, lead the students in a discussion about how a mystery author uses clues to lead the reader to the mystery's solution. Use a specific text, such as a short mystery, to illustrate this concept. Read the text and ask the students to listen (or look, if there are pictures) for the clues that the author left for the detective in the story and the reader of the mystery. Remind the students that when they search for clues, they are being detectives just like the detective character in the story. Make a poster with two headings: *What are the clues? How* will I use this clue to help me solve the mystery? Ask students to share the clues they found as they were listening and describe how the clues helped lead the reader to the mystery's solution. Record their thoughts on the chart.

After sharing, explain that just like clues help a detective solve a mystery, they can help a test taker *know what is important on a test*. Test authors use clues to help the reader recognize important information and to find the right answer.

Show a sample page overhead and lead a think-aloud about the clues that you find on that page and how they help you know what is important in that particular question. Examples of clues might be underlined, boxed, or capitalized text, and large or italicized font.

Student Practice:

Pair up students and pass out copies of practice test questions along with a paper that has two headings: *What are the clues? How will I use this clue to help me answer the question?* For example, students might write, "The words *sentence three* in question #2 are capitalized, so I know to pay close attention to that sentence as I'm reading the passage." Give the students time to find the author's clues and to decide how each clue helps them answer the question. Remind them to use the class chart generated during the demonstration as a resource.

Share:

After the students have finished, bring them back together and discuss their findings. Generate a class chart using their ideas.

In closing, write the following question on the board: How is a test taker like a detective? Allow students to share ideas and use this process as an assessment tool. Record this strategy, Use Author's Clues, on your Test-Taking Strategies anchor chart.

Assess:

Notice which students have not grasped the concept and allow time for reteaching during small groups. Finding authors' clues can be practiced with all types of texts across the curriculum.

• • •

STRATEGY

Identifying and following directions

There is so much text on a standardized test that it can be a challenge for students even to find the directions, much less follow them. It's important to review your specific test to determine how directions are presented. Some tests use larger font, italics, bold text, or boxed text.

Target Question:

Do I know how to find and use the directions to make the test easier?

Materials:

- Overheads of sample test directions
- Copies of different sample test directions and questions

Demonstration:

Start the lesson by playing a short game of Simon Says. Write the directions on the board as you say them. Ask the students to think about what they have to do during the game in order to be successful. After the game, discuss their ideas. Possible responses might be listening carefully, concentrating, and following directions. Allow this activity to be a springboard into a discussion of the importance of following directions. Explain to the students that the most important word in a direction is the word that tells you what to do—the verb or action word. Have the students find the verb in each direction on the board and underline it.

Write these two questions on the board: When is a time that you needed to follow directions? What happens if you don't follow directions carefully? Have students partner up and discuss and record their responses.

Explain that the directions on their standardized test are the best clues that the test authors give them. On the overhead, show examples of how the directions appear on the test. Draw special attention to the clues that the test authors use to emphasize importance. Practice circling each set of directions and underlining the verb in each separate direction. List all the verbs used in the directions on the board and explain that if the students know how to act out each of those verbs, just like in Simon Says, they know how to take the test and succeed.

Student Practice:

Now that they know how to find the directions on the test, the students need to practice finding and following them. Pass out copies of sample test directions and have students work with partners to find and circle the directions, underline the verbs, and follow the directions one at a time as they would if it were test day. Circulate to make sure that each student is practicing this skill accurately.

Share:

After students have had ample time to practice, come back together as a class and discuss answers to these two questions: How is following directions on the test like playing Simon Says? When are other times throughout our day that we can practice finding and following directions? Record this strategy on your Test-Taking Strategies anchor chart.

Assess:

Notice which students have not completely grasped the concept and allow for practice time during other subjects throughout the day.

• • •

"Rereading is the strategy that is most useful to readers of all ages. When given opportunities to reread material, readers' comprehension always goes up" (Sibberson and Szymusiak 2003, 70). Rereading for readers, writers, and test takers should not only be taught, but expected and

STRATEGY
Rereading saves the day

practiced consistently. It will be necessary to model rereading for many purposes: to help problem solve an unknown word, to confirm, to use context clues to understand the meaning of a word, to clear up confusions about a character, to bring attention back to the text after a distraction or daydreaming, and to understand text that doesn't make sense.

Target Question:
Do I know how to use rereading to make the test easier?

Materials:
- Test practice passage on transparency
- Sticky notes
- Just-right texts

Demonstration:
Tell the students that sometimes when you watch a movie at home on DVD, you get distracted. Then, when you turn your attention back to the movie, you don't know what is happening. Ask whether this has ever happened to them, and let them discuss what they do when this happens. If no one mentions backtracking the DVD, explain that you have to replay the movie to see what happened while you were distracted. Then suggest that rereading can serve the same purpose on a test. Rereading can not only help you when you are distracted but also help you for many other reasons. Explain that rereading will be the most important strategy they use when they take the test.

Choose one reason for rereading during the test to teach during this lesson. Read the practice passage transparency while sliding a pointer under the words. Think aloud as you reread. "Hmmm…I don't think I understand the last two sentences. I need to reread." Reread the sentences. "Oh, now I get it. I reread…because I didn't understand what I read." If this is the first time you have modeled rereading, you should split this up and do a single lesson or more for each reason your reread. For instance, teach one lesson about rereading for context clues and another lesson about rereading when something doesn't make sense. As you reread for each reason, think aloud about why you are rereading. "I reread…because…." Reiterate that rereading is the most useful test-taking strategy that students can use.

Student Practice:

Ask the students to find a trade book to read for a designated amount of time. While they are reading, they should use sticky notes to mark two places where they reread. Notify the students that later they will need to be prepared to share the parts of text that they reread and the reasons why.

Share:

Ask the students to come to a gathering area on the floor, sitting eye-to-eye and knee-to-knee with a partner. They should each share the two places where they reread and explain why. Encourage them to use the language you modeled during the shared reading. "I reread…because…." Listen and choose students to share out. Record a variety of reasons for rereading on a class chart entitled Rereading Saves the Day. Remind students that smart readers and smart test takers do a lot of rereading *and* that you *expect* them to use this strategy often. Record this strategy on the Test-Taking anchor chart.

Assess:

As the students share, notice who needs further intervention. Some students will need similar lessons modeled in a small group.

Stamina: An Additional General Reading Strategy

No matter a test taker's age or command of general reading strategies, sitting, reading, thinking, rereading, and answering questions for several hours, several days in a row, is tough. The harder all this is, the harder the test will be. So how can we make the physical experience of test taking easier for elementary students? Building reading and thinking stamina will help build test-taking stamina. If students can sit, read, reread, and think for long chunks of time, they will be better prepared to sit, read, reread, think, and answer questions when it is time to take a standardized test.

Building stamina by reading daily must start in kindergarten and continue throughout the grades. School communities need to make a commitment that every classroom will have a daily extended period of time for independent reading. Although building reading and thinking stamina in school is important for all students, it is especially important in communities where students may not have a consistent quiet time or place to read and think at home.

Independent reading may start with just five minutes at the beginning of kindergarten and slowly increase in time. In primary grades, teachers often combine independent reading with buddy reading to help extend the time during which children are reading books. As students move to the upper grades, buddy reading is replaced by longer blocks of time for independent reading only. Noel Ridge, a literacy consultant, suggests that children read a few different types of text during independent reading time. This practice helps prepare students for reading several different types of text during one standardized reading test. Keeping a daily log will help students monitor the variety of genres read.

Teaching students to build stamina involves modeling and high expectations. As you begin this process, role play selecting interesting "just right books" (books at a child's independent reading level). Next, show children how to select a place in the room to read (far away from their best friend). Think out loud as you model. "Hmmm...I think I will sit over here because I won't be distracted by my friends." You may also need to teach lessons on what to do when your mind wanders from your book to thinking about yesterday's soccer game. Even after routines are established, it is common for management issues to require readdressing throughout the year. If your students haven't done this before, start small and add a few minutes every day. Students' slow, steady work on stamina will pay off during testing season.

••• TEST-SPECIFIC READING STRATEGY LESSONS

STRATEGY

Navigating the structure of standardized tests

In order for a reader to understand a mystery, she must first understand the structure of the mystery genre. As she reads, she must be expecting to find a puzzle to solve and clues to follow. In the same way, a test taker must understand the structure of the test genre in order to be successful reading and navigating it.

Target Question:
Do I know how to read the special structure of the test genre?

Materials:
- Sample texts of different genres
- Chart paper
- Marker
- Transparency and hard copies of sample practice tests
- Transparency of a short mystery text

Demonstration:

Ask students about the names of genres that they read and write. List on chart paper. As you reread the chart, ask students to talk to a partner about the characteristics of each genre. You may need to model this first. List a few pertinent characteristics for each genre.

Explain that students will be learning about the test genre, which, like all genres, has specific characteristics that readers need to know and understand. Some of these characteristics help make the test easier to read, but others can be confusing or make reading the test harder. Show two or three overheads of pages from sample practice tests. Ask the students to look at each one and discuss with a partner what they notice about the structure of the test. Chart these ideas. The students may discover characteristics such as formal language, numbered lines or paragraphs, boldface directions, and boxed text.

Student Practice:

Hand out hard copies of each overhead to small groups of students. Ask them to reread the material and circle the parts of the format that seem easy or helpful, and to underline the parts that are confusing or difficult. As an example, use the overheads from the demonstration to circle numbered paragraphs and explain that the test authors used numbers so that readers could quickly refer back to a particular paragraph if needed. Next, underline a question that contains a chart or graph and explain that students have to read and understand the graphic organizer before they answer the question. As the students work, circulate and assist as needed.

Share:

After students are done, make a two-column chart and record what is easy and what is difficult about the test genre.

Assess:

Use the information garnered from the share session to plan for further lessons. Notice what was difficult for students and plan small- or whole-group lessons based on need.

• • •

STRATEGY

Eliminating answers that don't match

Most standardized reading tests are multiple-choice tests, meaning that they consist of questions followed by several answer choices. Often, at least one choice is clearly wrong because it has little to do with the question. When students are adept at identifying and eliminating the answer that obviously doesn't match, they heighten their chance at success on each question.

Target Question:

Do I know how to eliminate answers that don't match to make the test easier?

Materials:

- Objects to display
- Overheads of practice test questions

Demonstration:

Display a pencil, piece of chalk, dry erase marker, and piece of construction paper and ask students to decide which object is not associated with chalkboard use. After the students discuss the question, ask them to take objects away and explain why each is not a good choice. This concrete example prepares the students for the abstract concept of eliminating choices that don't match the question on tests.

After the students have had time to discuss this exercise, write the following question and answers on the board.

Which object is most likely used with a chalkboard?

A pencil
B piece of chalk

C dry erase marker

D piece of construction paper

Use the question on the board to think aloud about the process and the reasons for eliminating "stupid answers." Explain to students that eliminating stupid answers is just like finding the choices that don't match. We call them stupid answers because the children enjoy the novelty of using the word *stupid* in school; it gets them excited about using this strategy. Emphasize that this strategy will help students on tests. Demonstrate physically eliminating stupid answers on the board. As each choice is eliminated, have students explain why the choice is a stupid answer. Discuss that there will sometimes be more than one answer remaining. Students must choose the *best* answer. Repeat this process with a practice test question on an overhead.

As a class, create one or two standardized test questions connected to the content the students are studying. Generate possible answers to the question, including combinations of stupid answers, good answers, and best answers. Practice eliminating stupid answers that don't match the question.

If your state test allows for this, suggest that they can physically cross out the stupid answers right in the test booklet.

Student Practice:

Have students pair up and make up their own test questions related to appropriate curriculum. Explain that they should create four possible answers like the ones they created as a class.

Share:

Have each pair buddy up with another pair and exchange questions. Students should use the elimination strategy to determine answers. After they are finished, meet with the whole class and discuss what worked and what was hard. Record the strategy Eliminate Answers That Don't Match on your Test-Taking Strategies anchor chart.

Assess:

Notice students who need further instruction. Ensure that students are using this strategy independently as they practice test taking.

Many test takers are entitled to special accommodations, including having the test read aloud. This unique style of test taking requires different strategies than a typical test taker uses. This lesson and others like it may be taught to these students in a small group, but practicing listening skills is also useful for all students. (Lesson adapted from literacy consultant Maria Grabowsky.)

Target Question:
Do I know how to make the test easier by listening carefully?

Materials:
- Pencil
- Three-section chart

Demonstration:
Begin by connecting reasons that readers reread to reasons that listeners might need to "relisten." For example, a reader might reread because her mind wandered, and a listener might need to ask a speaker to repeat information for the same reason. Ask students to discuss and share in pairs. Explain that listeners also use strategies to help themselves listen better, such as asking the speaker to repeat and/or to clarify. Suggest that listening strategies can help them not only as test takers but in many aspects of life.

Ask the students to discuss with a buddy what they do to get ready to listen. Record their ideas at the top of a three section chart with the labels, Getting Ready to Listen, During Listening, and After Listening. As you record their ideas under the Getting Ready to Listen section, leave some blank space to continue the list at the end of the lesson. Repeat for the During Listening and After Listening sections of the chart.

Tell your students that they are going to participate in a listening exercise. In addition to participating, you want them to notice what they do as listeners while they are involved in the exercise.

Student Practice:

Tell the students that today they will be listening carefully as you describe a house. After you have finished describing the house twice, they will draw it from memory. They may not pick up their pencils until the description is over. Remind them not to be worried about being a perfect artist.

This house is tall and made of brick. It has two floors. The top floor has three windows, and the bottom floor has four windows. The front door is in the middle of the four windows on the bottom floor. To the left of the house, there is a tall apple tree with five apples on it. The roof is pointy and has three clouds above it.

Repeat and then tell the students to begin drawing the house.

Share:

Give the students an opportunity to briefly share their house drawings. Then ask them what was easy and what was hard about this exercise. What strategies helped them remember what to draw? What would have made the hard parts easier?

Redirect their attention to the three-section chart you used at the beginning of the lesson. Review each section: *Getting Ready to Listen*, *During Listening*, and *After Listening*. Ask the students to think about what they did during the house exercise and add their ideas to the chart. Record the strategy Actively Listen on your Test-Taking Strategies anchor chart.

Assess:

Notice which students' house drawings are far from complete. Did these students contribute to the chart? Which part of listening is easiest for them? Which part of listening is hardest for them? You may need to do further work in small groups on strategies for getting ready to listen, during listening, or after listening.

Next Steps:

In our experience, many students are timid about signaling their need to hear part of the test reread. Readers are permitted to reread if needed, and aural test takers should also feel empowered to signal their need to "relisten." After you and your colleagues have established a schoolwide signal for requesting rereading during a standardized test, provide plenty of opportunity to practice before testing season.

Additional Test-Specific Strategies

Not/Except

Some of the trickiest test questions are those that include the words *not* or *except*. These questions require the test taker to "think backward." An example follows:

Which of these strategies is *not* helpful to a reader?

A rereading
B predicting
C multiplying
D inferring

To be successful answering this type of question, students need to learn an effective strategy and practice using it. Michele Dusek, a fourth-grade teacher at Annandale Terrace, recommends the *T/F* strategy. She tells students to underline *not* or *except* when they see those words in a test question. As they read the answer choices, she teaches them to put a *T* by the choices that are true and *F* by the answers that are false. The answer choice that is false will be the best answer.

Another strategy is to skip the words *not* or *except* when they read, so that the question becomes, "Which of these strategies are helpful to a reader?" Then they can eliminate the helpful strategies, and the one that is left is the best answer.

Forget About It

Some students are so motivated to get every test question correct that when they face one they can't answer, they get too upset to move on.

These students resemble Olympic gymnasts who take a fall in the beginning of a routine and are never able to recover fully. In small groups, we teach these students to expect hard and confusing questions on tests. Smart test takers aren't necessarily sure of every single answer, but they are sure to read each question carefully, use strategies, make the very best answer choice, and move on confidently.

To help these students move on from a tough question, we teach them to tell themselves to "forget about it" (with or without the New York accent!) after they have gone through these steps—even if they are unsure they have answered correctly. Skipping tricky questions in hopes of going back to them later can cause frustration, confusion, and panic, especially if students are being timed or using bubble sheets.

Each class seems to have at least one student who falls into the perfectionist category. For that student, this strategy might mean the difference between success and utter frustration on standardized tests. Each class also has students who might overuse Forget About It, which is why we choose to identify small groups of students to learn this strategy instead of making it a whole-class lesson. Forget About It is an easy strategy for students to practice on homework and tests across the curriculum. For some, command of this strategy may make the entire school day less stressful.

Final Thoughts

When I gave up at the end of the cake debacle, I did the only thing that was in my power: I purchased cupcakes. In the absence of a teacher, I had no choice, no other strategy available. Teaching students to use a collection of both general and genre-specific strategies transfers power to students and offers options for success instead of a recipe for disaster.

3 | What's It All About? Finding the Main Idea

One night at bedtime, a teacher friend read *The Velveteen Rabbit* to her four-year-old son, Connor. As they finished the book, she asked Connor what he had learned from the story. Connor curled up with his blankie, eyes half-closed, and responded, "When stuff gets old and kinda smelly, you have to love it anyway. Like Grandpa." Connor was only four, but he knew that a message about life was woven into the story of the Velveteen Rabbit, and that this message could help him understand his world (and his poor grandpa) a little bit better. While his mother read, Connor was relating to the main character's feelings and making connections between the rabbit and his grandpa. By the end of the story, he had the main idea and its meaning in his own life all figured out, and his schema about unconditional love had been expanded a bit.

This is what a thoughtful reader does with a text: he lets the text meet him where he is and, in the end, drop him off in a new place by deepening his understanding, not just of the text, but of his own life. *Reading becomes growing* when the reader can look between the lines to find the main ideas, themes, and deeper meanings.

The process that a reader applies to a text to identify main ideas, or themes, is called determining importance. For nonfiction, this process includes differentiating between essential and extraneous text; for fiction, using schema along with the text to infer main ideas and themes. Since identifying main ideas is a fundamental reading skill that helps the reader understand and enjoy reading, it is heavily emphasized on standardized tests.

In testing this skill using fictional passages, standardized tests often challenge students to differentiate between the plot and theme of the passage. Students must know that the plot is the set of events that can be read chronologically in the story, while the themes are the big ideas that readers can infer from the text. In *Strategies that Work* (2000), Stephanie Harvey and Anne Goudvis describe themes this way: "Themes are the underlying ideas that give the story its texture, depth, and meaning. We infer themes. Themes often make us feel angry, sad, guilty, joyful, or frightened…we are likely to feel themes in our gut" (109). The ability to identify or generate the theme of a text requires a higher level of thinking than is required to recount a plot, and students must be offered plenty of practice before test day.

One of the confusing aspects of teaching and learning the concept of the main idea is that each resource book, teacher, and test seems to use different vocabulary. This is why it is imperative to use the specific language of your test during the unit of study, and why the test talk lessons connected with this skill are crucial. Keep in mind that even if a student is a whiz at finding the main ideas within texts, your state won't recognize her knowledge if the student can't identify the main idea questions *within the test* because it uses different vocabulary than you did in your classroom. For consistency throughout this chapter, we use the terms *theme* and *main idea* interchangeably to describe the underlying meanings and lessons within fiction and nonfiction texts. Here is an example of how a third-grade teacher introduced her unit on determining importance to find the main ideas.

Beginning a Unit About Main Idea

It's mid-October in Glennon's third-grade reading workshop. The class has just completed a unit of study about recounting the plot of a text. Today the students will begin a unit about finding the main idea in fiction. The children are gathered at her feet, listening intently to their third Patricia Polacco book of the week, *Thank You, Mr. Falker* (1998). It is the story of a girl named Tricia who moves to a new school and struggles to learn to read. The students alternate between listening to Glennon read and reflecting on the text with a partner when she stops to ask discussion questions. After she is finished reading the text, Glennon draws a chart on the board and titles the first column Plot and the second column Themes/ Main Ideas. She reminds the students that plot is the set of events that happen in a story or passage and can be found right in the text. She asks the students to recount the plot of *Thank You, Mr. Falker* to her, and she records the events in sequential order in the first column.

Glennon then turns her attention to the second column and connects students' background knowledge to the new concept by saying, "Since you are experts about finding the plot of a text, today we are going to move ahead and start learning about another very important part of a text called the main idea or theme. The main ideas are the big ideas or lessons that the author wants us to think about and learn from his or her text. This is a really important skill to have because it helps us understand and enjoy our reading, and it is also a skill that the SOL will test you on at the end of the year. Let's figure out how to find the main ideas together. Remember when we studied finding the plot of a story or a test passage? Can anyone think aloud with me about what you do when you have to find the plot of a passage, like on the SOL?"

B.J. raises his hand and says, "I just start at the beginning and try to think of everything that I read. It's really easy."

"Finding the plot *is* pretty easy, isn't it? To find the plot of a text, we simply recount the events that the author included in the text. But finding the main ideas is trickier because they are not usually written right in the text. We have to read and then use our schema with the text to *infer* the main ideas. We have to think about the characters and their feelings more. How do you think Tricia felt when her mom told her they were moving?"

Ahmed raises his hand and says, "I think Tricia felt scared that her new class would make fun of her because she doesn't know how to read." Glennon has modeled quality talk all year; she teaches her students to speak in complete sentences and support opinions with evidence from the text. The other students nod in agreement with Ahmed's thought and Glennon records his comment in a notebook.

Next, she rereads a passage in which a bully named Eric is teasing Tricia about her difficulty with reading. She pauses to say, "Turn to a partner and discuss your thoughts about the way Eric is behaving toward Tricia." After the students have discussed, she rereads the last page of the book and says, "Talk to your partner one more time about what you think Patricia Polacco would want her readers to learn from this book." During each of the partner discussion times, Glennon circulates among her students and records their ideas in her notebook to be used during the next part of the lesson.

Glennon directs the students back to the chart at the front of the room. She writes the word *fear* in the Main Ideas column and says, "Ahmed's idea was that Tricia was afraid that her new class would laugh at her. Does anyone have a connection with that?" Glennon's first unit of study this year was about becoming better readers by making connections to text.

Giselle responds, "I have a connection with that. I know how Tricia felt because I was scared when I came here from my country. I didn't think anyone would speak my language." Glennon writes *fear of being different* on the chart paper.

"I heard Nancy tell her partner that Eric was jealous of Tricia because Mr. Falker seemed to like her drawing," Glennon adds. She writes the word *jealousy* on the chart paper and asks, "Who can connect with jealousy?"

"I felt jealous when my baby sister was born. I felt like my parents would forget about me,"says Rokshar. Other students show their connections to Rokshar's comment by nodding.

Michael raises his hand. "I think it is cool that Tricia can't read but can draw really well, and Eric can read but can't draw well," he says.

Mark agrees. "Yeah, everyone has things they are good at and things that they need help with." Glennon writes *strengths and weaknesses* on the chart paper.

Then Glennon asks, "What do you think Patricia Polacco wants us to know or learn about life from her book *Thank You, Mr. Falker*? What were the main ideas in the book? Use our list and the text-to-self connections you made while we read to help you." Students partner-talk and then share ideas such as fear, family love, and learning not to give up. Glennon concludes by connecting their ideas and discussion to the test once again. At the bottom of the chart, she creates a multiple-choice question in the same format the SOL uses.

Which is NOT a main idea in Patricia Pollacco's *Thank You, Mr. Falker*?

A fear
B jealousy
C strengths and weaknesses
D sportsmanship

Glennon encourages the students to use their test-taking strategies to navigate the question, and, after they have answered, she asks, "Why is it important to be able to find the main ideas in a text, beside the fact that it will be on our SOLS?" The class giggles and Bo Hyun raises her hand. "Because reading a story is sometimes like learning a lesson," she says. "If you can't find the main idea, you don't get the lesson!"

Glennon reinforces his thinking. "That's so smart! When readers read fiction and test takers read passages, they can't just read the text. They have to use their schema and their hearts to decide what the author wanted them to learn or think about. Sometimes tests call this the *main idea* or *theme*. We'll learn more about this tomorrow."

Wrapping It Up: Test Talk Lesson

Today is the last lesson of Glennon's unit on main idea. At the end of this school year, her students will take the required state standardized test for the first time, so Glennon plans to spend the last one or two days of each unit connecting what they have learned to the specific language on the test. At the end of a three-week, in-depth unit of study, most of her students are now experts on the terms *determining importance, big idea, main idea,* and *theme*. Glennon's objective for this lesson is to ensure that her students are familiar with the format and vocabulary the SOL will use to ask about this concept. Today she will help the children translate what they have learned into test talk. In reviewing past tests while planning this lesson, she has found main idea questions asked several different ways: What is the main idea of this story? Which sentence from the story best states its main idea? What is this passage mainly about? What does the author of this passage want the reader to know? What is this story mostly about?

Because these students have not seen the test before, Glennon begins the lesson by distributing a few pages of the released items from last year's state test. She asks the students to browse through the pages with partners and talk about what they notice. Right away, Glennon observes that the students look confused. Oscar raises his hand and says, "I don't get what the questions are asking."

Giselle adds, "I don't understand the directions, and these words are really hard!"

Glennon responds, "Which question are you looking at that you don't understand?"

Cesar looks at his test and says "Number 5 says, 'What is this passage mainly about?'"

Glennon says, "That question means, 'What is the big idea of the text?'"

Sakshi calls out, "Well, why don't they just say it that way? I would have known the answer if they asked it the way you did."

"I think you have discovered the trickiest thing about the test," Glennon replies. "It seems to be written in a different language then we're used to, doesn't it?"

Glennon asks the students to continue their partner talk. After a few minutes, Mark says, "Abu and I decided that it really isn't fair. This test doesn't make sense to us because the words are too confusing!"

Glennon reassures the class. "You're right. The test is written in a language we aren't used to. Let's call it 'test talk.' Here's the great news! By the time the test comes along you will have learned even more than you'll need to know to pass this test. You will know how to translate the test talk to language you understand. Many of you are used to translating one language to another already, and I am going to teach you how to use that skill on the test."

The next day, Glennon hands out the released items packets again. She asks her students to read through the questions and copy on sticky notes at least two questions that they think relate to determining importance or finding the big idea. When they are done, the class comes together in a circle to share. Glennon makes an anchor chart titled Main Idea Test Talk. The partners come up one at a time and present their ideas.

Ahmed says, "Number 4 asks, 'Which best states the main idea of the passage?' We think that this is about big idea because it says *main idea* in it, and those are the same. *Main* means important, like how the main characters in a story are the most important ones." After Glennon copies number 4 onto the chart, Ahmed continues, "We didn't know what the rest of the words in that question meant, though."

Glennon asks, "Which words are confusing you?"

Joseph replies, "The first part is confusing. 'Which best states' doesn't make sense to me."

Glennon stops to explain. "*States* has many different meanings. In this question, *states* is a synonym for a word you know well. Let's try to figure it out together." She writes a sentence on the white board: *Julia walks in the classroom and states, "It's time for art."* Glennon underlines the word *states* and asks the kids to use the context to figure out the well-known synonym. Sarah replies, "It is the same as *says* or *said*."

"That's right, Sarah. Would you like to add those two words to our synonym chart from word study?" Glennon's class will translate similar generic test talk to kid talk throughout the year on a synonym chart, but today she wants to focus specifically on test talk involving the main idea.

Diego and Rashid are next. "Number 10 asks, 'What is this passage mostly about?' We think that's about big idea because *mostly about* is kind of like *theme*. It's what the author wants you to know the most. We don't really know what *passage* means though." Glennon explains that *passage* is the same as *text*, a term with which the students are familiar. She suggests that Diego can add *passage* and *text* to the class synonym chart after the lesson.

The class continues to share while Glennon adds the test talk to the Main Idea Test Talk chart. Mario is excited to share his discovery. "Number 8 asks, 'Where does this story most likely take place?' That one is about main idea because it is about *most* and that is the same as *main*."

Glennon says, "Thanks, Mario. Let's double-check the words in the question to make sure it is about main idea. How about *take place*? What is that asking about?"

Diego says, "*Takes place* means where something happens, like lunch takes place in the cafeteria."

"Good job. Questions with *takes place* are about setting, not main idea." The students continue to discover and discuss the main idea test talk, and Glennon records it on the chart. When the lesson is completed, she puts the anchor chart on the classroom wall to be used as a resource until test time.

● ● ●   **CONCEPT REVIEW LESSON**

STRATEGY

Identifying the main idea of an illustration

Target Question:
Can I decide what is important in a picture and use this information to find the main idea?

Materials:
- *Wilma Unlimited: How Wilma Rudolph Became the World's Fastest Woman* (Krull 1996)

- Color transparency of pages two and twelve
- Chart paper

Demonstration:

The teacher gathers the class for a mini-lesson. She writes *determining importance*, *main idea*, and *theme* on the board and asks the students to talk to a partner about what these terms mean. After they share out, she asks them to discuss how these concepts are similar and how they are connected. (Determining importance in texts leads us to the main ideas and themes.)

After some discussion about these terms, the teacher tells the class that knowing what's important and what is just a detail in a piece of art is similar to determining importance in text; it helps us find the main idea and understand the artist's message more deeply. To activate the students' schema about main idea and have some fun, they will be discussing how to find the main idea in a piece of art. The teacher puts the transparency of page two from *Wilma Unlimited* on the overhead projector and gives the students time to look and think. She creates a chart titled What Questions Do I Ask Myself to Find the Main Idea of a Picture? Underneath the title, she makes two columns and titles the first column What Does the Artist Want Me to Think Is Important? The teacher thinks aloud about what looks important in the picture, such as the mother, the little girl, the birthday cake, and the way the family seems focused on the little girl. She records these ideas in the first column. She then discusses the details that are interesting but don't necessarily support the main idea of the picture. These details might include the family's apparel and the background of the picture. In thinking aloud about the clues she uses to determine what is important and what is not, the teacher refers to things like light, color, positioning, and size.

Next the teacher records the second question she asks herself to determine the main idea of the picture: What Can I Learn From This Picture? She allows students time to share ideas and charts their responses (take care of your family, stay close to those you love, celebrate important events together, etc.).

The teacher tells the class that the answers to these questions help the audience determine the main idea. She explains that she thinks some of the themes or main ideas of the illustration are celebration, adoration, family love and closeness, support, and mother/daughter bond. She records these main ideas at the bottom of the chart and demonstrates how the information in the two columns leads her to conclusions about the main idea.

Student Practice:
The teacher tells the students that they will now get a chance to determine importance to find the main idea of a picture. Each pair receives a copy of page twelve of *Wilma Unlimited*. The teacher asks them to use the pictures and the questions from the chart to help them find the main ideas in the illustration. Students struggling with this process should be paired with those who feel more confident.

Share:
The teacher asks each pair to share their ideas with another pair. Finally, the whole class comes together to discuss what was easy and what was hard about this process. In preparation for tomorrow's lesson, she asks students what they think is the same about finding the main idea of a picture and of a text.

Assess:
The teacher notices students who need more help and meets with them to reteach the concept before beginning the next lesson.

• • •   CONCEPT REVIEW LESSON

STRATEGY

Identifying main idea in a poem

Target Question:
Do I remember how to identify the main idea of a poem?

Materials:
- Transparency of demonstration poem, "When I Am Full of Silence" (Prelutsky 1994)
- Copies and transparency of student practice poem, "Listen" (Grimes 1997)
- Chart paper

Demonstration:

The teacher calls the class together and writes this question on the board: What questions do I ask myself to determine the main idea of an illustration? She asks the students to think back to yesterday's lesson, turn to a buddy, and share responses. The teacher refers them to the anchor chart from yesterday's lesson to help with their partner discussion. Next, she tells the students that today they will be using similar strategies to find the main idea of a poem, something they will be required to do on the state test.

The teacher puts the poem "When I Am Full of Silence" on the overhead projector. She rereads the poem several times and then begins to think aloud about finding the main idea. She refers to the chart from yesterday's lesson and begins a new chart titled What Questions Do I Ask Myself to Find the Main Idea of a Poem?

The teacher begins a think-aloud about finding the main idea of a poem. It might sound like this: "When I read a poem, I use all the words to make a picture in my head that matches what the poet is trying to say. You'll remember from our poetry unit that this is called *visualization*. As I read this poem, I visualize myself as a child in my special quiet place, away from my big brothers and sister. Just like the poet, I liked this time because I didn't have to listen to anyone else, and the only voice I heard was my own. This helps me connect to the poem, which helps me understand the main idea.

"So the first question I ask myself to find the main idea of a poem is 'What do I visualize when I read this poem?'" The teacher records this question and her visualizations on the chart. After she gives the students a chance to practice visualizing on their own, she continues, "After I visualize, I ask myself, 'What does the poet want me to learn from this poem?'" She records this question in the second column and asks the students to reread the poem and discuss possible answers with a partner.

Next the teacher shares and records her response to the second question: "The poet wants me to learn that it's OK to take time for myself, and that sometimes quiet time can help me think and know myself better." She asks for other ideas from students and records them under her response.

Finally, the teacher shows the students how the information gathered in the two columns helps her determine the main ideas or themes of the poem. Possible main ideas are the value of privacy, self-awareness, and independent thinking.

When I Am Full of Silence
by Jack Prelutsky (1994)

When I am full of silence,
and no one else is near,
the voice I keep inside me
is all I want to hear.
I settle in my secret place,
contented and alone,
and think no other thoughts except
the thoughts that are my own.

When I am full of silence,
I do not want to play,
to run and jump and fuss about,
the way I do all day.
The pictures painted in my mind
are all I need to see
when I am full of silence...
when I am truly me.

Student Practice:

The teacher puts students into groups of three or four and gives each group a poem. She asks the groups to read the poem and answer the questions modeled in the lesson in order to determine the poem's main idea. She reminds students to use the anchor chart as a resource and stresses the importance of each group member contributing ideas.

STUDENT PRACTICE POEM:

Listen
by Nikki Grimes (1997)

Listen:
Let me tell you
where things stand.
Each day is like fruit
Resting ripe in my hand.
Will I sample its sweetness?

Will I toss it away?
Will I let you steal it?
I got one thing to say:
Don't try it.
Don't try it.

Share:

As students gather, the teacher places a transparency of the poem on the overhead. She reads it aloud and asks volunteers to discuss their group's process in finding the main idea. The teacher reminds students that the test will require them to identify the main ideas of many different text types, not just poetry. After students have shared their thinking, the teacher might ask some assessment questions: How is finding the main idea of a poem different or the same as finding the main idea of a picture? Why is it important to be able to find the main idea of a poem? What other types of texts might we be asked to find the main idea of on our test? How will finding the main ideas of those text types differ from today's process?

Assess:

The teacher notices students who need further intervention.

Further Steps:

- In writing workshop, ask students to identify the themes and main ideas in their own writing.
- Practice finding the main idea in different text types, including non-fiction.
- For homework, ask students to identify the main ideas of the TV shows and movies they watch.

TEST TALK LESSON   • • •

Target Question:

Can I find and understand main idea test talk?

Materials:

- Main Idea Test Talk anchor chart from main idea unit of study (If

STRATEGY

Identifying main idea test talk

you haven't created one yet, prepare a chart for this lesson.)

- • Overhead of sample test passage with a sample question about main idea
- • Copies of sample passages of various text types for group practice work

(Sample passage and question should mirror those on your test as closely as possible.)

Demonstration:

Unless you are teaching this lesson at the end of your first unit of study, it should not be the students' first introduction to the concept of test talk. Please see page 44 for ideas about how to expose students to this idea.

The teacher begins by reminding the students that in order to show what they know about main idea on the reading test, they will need to be able to identify the main idea questions and translate the test talk that those questions use. She puts a transparency of the sample passage and accompanying multiple-choice questions on the overhead. As she reads, she focuses not on answering the question, but on the tricky language, or test talk, within the question and answer choices, along with the best test-taking strategies to use on questions that concern main idea.

The teacher first asks the students to refer to the Main Idea Test Talk anchor chart to help them answer this question: what test talk do the test writers use to let me know they are asking about the main idea of a passage? Students will notice that the question and answer choices might contain language like *summarize*, *theme*, *mostly about*, etc. The teacher circles the language that the students identify as test talk within the passage, question, and answer choices. After the students understand how to use the test talk to identify a main idea question, the teacher asks, "What verbs do the test takers use to give me clues about what to do in this question?" Answers may include *find*, *locate*, *determine*, *decide*, etc. As the teacher underlines, the class discusses how these verbs can help the test taker determine what to do with the passage and thus lead him to the best answer. Finally, the teacher refers to the Test-Taking Strategies anchor chart and asks, "Which test-taking strategies will help me answer this question?" Students might respond with various helpful strategies like elimination and rereading, etc.

Student Practice: Be the Test Author Game

Today students will get a chance to be the test writers. Pairs of students are given sample passages and asked to read the passage and then develop one or two main idea questions using the language of the test, or test talk. They can refer to the Main Idea Test Talk anchor chart. When they are finished, each pair trades its passage and question with another pair, who reads and answers it. Remind students to use test-taking strategies when answering the questions. When they finish, foursomes get together and see if they were successful in choosing the right answer.

Share:

Students share their questions and answers with the class. The teacher ensures that all the language from the anchor chart has been discussed.

Assess:

During practice and share time, the teacher circulates and takes note of students who are not able to identify test talk, verbs, or strategies. Finding time to reteach during small group or individual conferences is crucial, as the entire review will build upon these skills as it progresses.

PRACTICE WITH TEXTS LESSON

• • •

Target Question:

Can I use my knowledge of main idea, main idea test talk, and test-taking strategies to answer a multiple-choice question?

Materials:

- Transparency of demonstration poem "Change" (Bishop 1999) and accompanying question
- Several copies each of student practice poems "Listen to the Mustn'ts," "Early Bird," "Tree House," and "Helping" (These poems are all from *Where the Sidewalk Ends* [Silverstein 1974], a book found in every school library.)

STRATEGY

Synthesizing content, test talk, and test-taking knowledge

- Copies of student practice multiple-choice questions
- Transparencies of student practice poems

Demonstration:

The teacher tells students that today they will combine all of their knowledge about main idea, main idea test talk, and test-taking strategies to see if they can answer a test question. Before they try on their own, she will lead a think-aloud to demonstrate how a smart test taker attacks a question. She puts the Main Idea Test Talk anchor chart and the Test-Taking Strategies chart on the board to use as references. Using a transparency of "Changes," the demonstration poem, on the overhead, she begins a think-aloud that might sound like this:

"The first thing I notice about this test page is that there are directions at the top. I know that I should always read directions carefully, so I'll do that first. I'm going to underline the verbs because that will help me remember what the test writers want me to do. The directions also tell me that this passage will be a poem, and that there will be a question about the poem afterward. I think I'll read the poem once first and then check out the questions so I know what I'm looking for when I reread."

The teacher reads the poem once and then reads the question: "The question says, 'This poem is mainly about . . .' Hmmm . . . oh, I remember that *mainly about* is just like *mostly about*. That's test talk for main idea! I'm going to circle the test talk and even write *main idea* next to it. Great! I know how to find the main idea of a poem. I'd better read this one a few more times so I can ask myself what I visualize when I read and what the author wants me to learn from the poem. I know that answering those questions will lead me to the main idea."

The teacher rereads the poem several times, discussing her visualizations and the main idea the poet is trying to convey. She then moves on to the answer choices, using strategies such as elimination and rereading to isolate the best answer.

DEMONSTRATION POEM:

Read the following poem and use it to answer #4.

Change

by Rudine Bishop (1999)

There's been the strangest kind of change
Since autumn came into the woods.
The mountain maples' summer hats
Have turned to bright red riding hoods.

4. This poem is mainly about

    A the Little Red Riding Hood fairy tale.

    B the way mountains looks as autumn changes to winter.

    C the color change of the leaves when summer turns to autumn.

    D seasonal changes.

Student Practice:

The teacher asks students to partner up, then passes out the practice poems and questions. Students work together to identify the main idea test talk, read and discuss the main ideas of each poem, and use test-taking strategies to find the best answer. The teacher reminds students to use the process modeled in the demonstration. (The questions below refer to the Shel Silverstein poems listed in the Materials section above.)

STUDENT PRACTICE

Which best states the main idea of "Listen to the Mustnt's"?

    A Listen closely to adults.

    B Don't try to make your dreams come true.

    C You can do anything that you decide to do.

    D Don't listen to what adults say.

Which of the following is a theme of "Early Bird"?

    A Birds and worms are friends.

    B Stay up late.

    C The early bird gets the worm.

    D Worms are lazy.

The poem "Tree House" is mostly about

    A how a house is boring.

    B how a tree house is the best kind of house.

    C how building a tree house is hard.

    D why a street house is better than a tree house.

What is the main idea of the poem "Helping"?

    A Friends should help each other.

    B You should help people only when they ask.

    C All the people in the poem are good friends, except Zachary Zugg.

    D None of the above.

Share:

The teacher shows each poem on the overhead, and each group discusses the process it went through to find the main idea: identifying the test talk, visualizing the poem, and discussing what the poet wanted the reader to learn. Finally, each group shares the test-taking strategies it used to isolate the best answer.

Assess:

The teacher makes time for small-group work, with other poems and texts, for students who are still struggling with the concept of main idea.

Further Steps:

Model finding the main idea with the different kinds of texts that will appear on your state's test. Explore how the questions that readers have to ask themselves to find the main idea of various text types differ. For example, what questions do readers ask themselves to find the main idea in a fictional passage? A nonfiction passage?

Recently my neighbor Sarah, with whom I rarely get a chance to talk, called me on the phone. She had just given birth to twins, and after sharing a few stories about the chaos at her house, she said good-bye and we hung up. That evening at dinner I told my husband that since Sarah and I don't normally socialize, I thought the call odd because there didn't seem to be a reason for it. My husband said, "Maybe Sarah's lonely, or maybe she was hoping you'd offer to help with the kids, or maybe she just dialed the wrong number and thought you were somebody else." Hoping that the wrong number theory wasn't correct, I called Sarah back and offered to babysit the twins one afternoon. She chuckled and told me that asking for help had in fact been the purpose of her call, but she had lost her nerve on the phone. We had a laugh and agreed that next time, we'd not waste our time with small talk and get straight to our motives!

Like that phone call, any communication gets confusing when you don't understand its purpose. Simply defined, writing is one person's *purposeful attempt to communicate* with another. Since all modes of communication, including writing, are generated by a specific goal, knowing the messenger's purpose is crucial to understanding his message.

When a reader can determine a writer's purpose, a relationship develops between writer and reader, and the text comes alive. The reader is able to imagine the writer and to use his textual clues and tone to consider his motives. As students become active citizens, the ability to read critically will become crucial in their attempt to make sense of the world. They must be able to approach every editorial, advertisement, and periodical with a critical eye, determining the writer's position and agenda before deciding upon the validity of his message. As an old saying goes, "There is no reality, only perception." It is the responsibility of every reader and citizen not to accept every text as truth, but to see it as one writer's perception of the truth. Readers can make this distinction when they are able to filter the author's purpose from the text. This is an incredibly important reading skill, one that can be difficult for students to learn without lots of modeling and practice.

After we have taught our students how to identify an author's intent, another challenge arises. Even a student who has mastered this skill may find questions about it on standardized tests to be challenging. This is because the test talk that is linked to author's intent is often more varied than in any other kind of test question. A student may be able to identify that a passage's purpose is to persuade, but does he also know that *encourage*, *advertise*, *negotiate*, *influence*, *convince*, *warn*, and *prove* are all synonyms often used to describe a persuasive text? Author's intent questions may evaluate a student's vocabulary and language flexibility more than any other question type. These questions can be especially frustrating for students with limited exposure to English. In order for students to be successful with author's intent questions, they must be taught not only the skill but also the varied language that is used by tests to describe an author's intent.

Beginning a Unit About Author's Intent

Michelle Jones, a third-grade teacher, is preparing to begin a unit of study about author's intent. Her goal is to help her students become more critical readers by using different text types to learn to identify an author's intent. She knows she must also teach her state's objectives in a creative and concrete way, helping her students learn and recognize the language that the test will use. After spending hours researching past tests, she is ready to begin the unit, meshing her expectations with the test's expectations of her students as readers and learners.

Just before lunch, the third graders have completed read-aloud and are sitting in a circle waiting for Michelle's next direction. She begins, "After lunch today, we will begin an exciting new unit during reading workshop. Before we can get started, though, you have a job to do at lunch to help you prepare." She passes out note cards and pencils and continues, "Today at lunch you have an extra responsibility in addition to following directions and being respectful. Today I need you to record three things that you say to your friends in the cafeteria. For example, if I am sitting at the lunch table and I say, 'Can I have some ketchup?' I should write that down on my note card. If you are feeling quiet today and you would prefer to write down what someone else says, that's fine too. Please don't worry about spelling: just do the best you can. Are there any questions?" The students glance around at one another, pleased with their lunchtime challenge.

When the students arrive back in the classroom after lunch, Michelle asks them to come to the carpet with their note cards. She puts a two-column chart on the board with the first column titled What We Said. Michelle asks for volunteers to share what they recorded. Examples include:

"I lost my pencil. Can I borrow yours?"
"I need a napkin."
"I went out to dinner with my parents last night."
"Joni told me a cool joke. Wanna hear it?"
"Don't blow into your milk or you'll get in trouble!"
"You should trade me your cookie for my nuggets."

She records these quotes and continues, "It looks like you all had a lot to communicate to one another at lunch today. Why do you suppose that you use so many words to talk to one another at lunch instead of sitting silently?" Sarah raises her hand and says, "That would be boring!"

Malik agrees. "Also, if you forget something in line, you have to ask for it or you'd end up with no ketchup."

Michelle smiles and says, "It sounds like there are a lot of reasons that we speak to one another. Sarah says things would be boring if we didn't talk, and Malik says we wouldn't get what we want or need. Let's look at the things you said at lunch and try to decide *why* you said them." She titles the second column Why We Said It. The students reread the quotes and record many reasons for their communication, including "needed something," "trying to make people laugh," "trying to get information," "giving information," "warning someone," and "trying to get someone to do something."

After they collect their list, Michelle says, "It seems that you all are very effective at communicating through words for lots of different reasons. Can you think of any other ways that people communicate?"

Lisa raises her hand and says, "Some people make mean faces when they are communicating that they're mad."

"Great! Facial expressions are another way to communicate. Anything else?"

Jose says, "Some people write to communicate."

"You are right, Jose. People write for all different reasons, just like people talk for all different reasons. Today we are going to start learning how to decide why authors write certain texts. Just like finding the main idea, finding the author's reason for writing helps us understand our reading better. Authors write for many of the same reasons that we talk. On the SOL test, you will be asked to decide why authors wrote certain passages. Those reasons are called the author's intent, and at the end of this unit, you will be experts on finding the author's intent."

To conclude the introductory lesson, Michelle writes a multiple-choice question on the board. "Right now, find a partner and answer this question using your test-taking strategies," she says. "In a few minutes I'll ask you to share the process you used to answer." Here is the question:

What is the reason that the test authors write the *reading* test?

    A to drive us crazy
    B to make sure that we are learning how to become good readers
    C because they are bored
    D because they want to make sure we are paying attention during math

The students partner up and discuss the question. Michelle circulates and listens to the discussions. When she hears Jose tell his partner, "The author must have thought the word *reading* was important because he wrote it in bold letters," she stops and says, "That is smart thinking, Jose! You are using the author's clues as a test-taking strategy. Would you share that thinking with the class when we come back together?" Jose beams and agrees to share.

Two minutes later, Michelle stops the class by asking, "Who would like to share their answering process?"

Jose raises his hand and begins. "First, Sara and I read the question. We noticed an author's clue. The word *reading* is in bold letters so the author must have thought it was important. We underlined that word. Then we read the answers and eliminated the stupid answers. We thought A and C were stupid."

Michelle stops Jose and says, "Wow, you've already used three strategies: reading carefully, looking for author's clues, and eliminating stupid answers. That's fantastic! Did anyone else use those strategies?" The students raise their hands and nod. Michelle says, "Now it looks like we are left with two good choices: B and D. Sara, how did you and Jose decide between those choices?"

"We looked at the question again and decided that reading was an important part of the question, so we knew the answer had to be about reading too," Sara says. "We also knew that the test author's reason for writing the reading test wouldn't be to see if we were good at math!" The other kids giggle and nod in agreement.

Michelle concludes, "That is such great thinking. You are already learning about why authors write, and tomorrow we will continue our learning by looking at some special texts and deciding the author's intent for writing them. Now you can go back to your seats and start your independent reading time. While you're reading your book, find the author's name and think about why he or she may have written the book. That's what we'll talk about during share time today. You can get started now."

Wrapping It Up: Test Talk Lesson

It is the last day of Michelle's author's intent unit of study. The class has spent three weeks in reading workshop exploring the purposes of different text types as well as the specific characteristics that are clues to those purposes. For example, the class spent one week exploring informative texts and learning that they usually intend to explain something or give information to the reader. As Michelle supported the students' independent research about informative texts, they discovered that when an author intends to inform, he or she might include facts, dates, or names. The students have become experts on finding clues or characteristics like these that help them to decide what type a certain text is. They know that identifying the text type will lead them to the author's purpose. Through assessments like one-on-one conferences, discussions in reading groups, and written and verbal quizzes, Michelle is confident that most of her students have a solid grasp on this concept as a reading skill.

Today she will teach the students to transfer their new knowledge about author's intent to the test by ending the unit with a test talk lesson.

Her students are comfortable with the format of this lesson and with the concept of test talk because this is the way they end every reading workshop unit of study. Michelle has thoroughly reviewed her state's released items from the last five years and has discovered that the different vocabulary and format the test uses to address this skill vary greatly. For this reason, she has decided to spend two days on author's intent test talk.

Michelle begins, "Today is the end of our author's intent unit. Who can tell me what we will be learning today?"

All hands are in the air, and Maria is called upon. "We're going to learn what words the SOL test will use to try to trick us about author's purpose."

"Right!" Michelle says. "Today we will learn to identify test talk for author's purpose questions. We know that it doesn't matter to the test how much we know if we can't show our knowledge by translating test talk. Let's start by briefly activating our schema about author's purpose. Why is it important for us to be able to read a text and identify the author's purpose for writing it?"

"Since it helps us understand reading better, there's gonna be lots of questions about it on the SOL," says Thomas.

"That's very smart! We know *why* it's important to find the author's purpose, but when we read a text, *how* do we find it? Turn to your neighbor and discuss that process."

After a few minutes of discussion, Michelle asks for volunteers to share out. Jennifer volunteers, "Karen and I decided that first you have to read a text and find clues to help you decide what kind of text type it is. Like if it sounds like the author's trying to get you to think a certain way, or if the text sounds like an argument, then it might be persuasive text. After you figure out what the text type is, it's easy to know the author's purpose. Like persuasive texts are usually written to change your mind or get you to do something."

"Wow! Sounds like you know how to find the author's intent. Today we better learn how to find the *questions* about author's intent on the SOL so you can prove what you know on the test. How will we learn which questions are about author's intent?"

"Let's hunt for them on the tests and make an author's intent test talk chart," suggests Joseph.

Michelle asks the students to partner up and passes out different versions of released test items from recent years. She gives her students stacks of sticky notes to mark the questions that they think ask about author's intent. The students hunt diligently and discuss which questions might or might not be about author's intent, while Michelle circulates to ensure that the students stay on task and on track. At the end of the allotted time, Michelle asks the students to come to the carpet to share, but many hands shoot into the air to request more time.

Thomas says, "Kevin and I are only halfway done because there are *tons* of author's purpose questions." The other students signal their agreement, and Michelle, pleased with their focus and quality talk, allows them ten more minutes for hunting. Afterward, the students return to the carpet with their partners and materials.

Michelle begins share time by asking an open-ended question that won't limit the students' thinking or responses. "What did you notice during your investigation of the test?"

Ahmed responds, "Kayla and I noticed that there are a million questions about author's purpose."

Kayla adds, "And we could find the author's intent questions, but some of the test talk in the answer choices was really hard."

"Kristen and I noticed that too," Jennifer says. "We also noticed that some questions are about the author's reason for writing the whole thing, and some questions are about why the author wrote one sentence or paragraph or something. That is like what we learned last week."

Michelle says, "It sounds like you're saying that today we need to pay attention to the author's intent test talk in the questions *and* the answer choices. We should also discuss the difference between finding the author's purpose for a whole passage or just for a sentence or paragraph. Let's get started! Why don't we make one chart with all the different questions you found that ask about author's purpose, and later we'll make a chart with all the test talk in the answers."

At the end of this share time, the class has created two charts:

Test Talk for Author's Intent Questions
Questions About Whole Passages

The author most likely wrote this passage to…
The poet most likely wrote this poem to…

The author both entertains and informs the reader by…
What was the author's main purpose for writing this article?
The author probably wrote this article in order to…
The author probably wrote this poem in order to…
The author's purpose in writing this passage was most likely to…

Questions About Parts of Passages

The author included the last paragraph because it…
The author included the first two paragraphs in this passage in
      order to…
In the last paragraph the author uses words that…
The reason the author uses the phrase "cool as a cucumber" is to…
Why does the author use words like *jump* or *race*?

"Wow! This is a lot of test talk that you've collected! Do you believe that the test uses this many different words to ask you about the same skill? Today we have learned that there are two different ways that the test might ask you about author's intent. It might ask what the purpose of a whole text is, or what the author's purpose was for adding a particular part of a text. We have also learned different test talk for questions about author's intent, so we'll know how to find these questions on the test. Great job! Tomorrow we will look at the author's intent test talk in the answer choices, and we'll learn how we can use that test talk to give us clues to find the right answers."

Author's Intent Test Talk Lesson: Day Two

It's day two of Michelle's author's intent test talk lesson. The students are sitting at their desks as Michelle begins. "Yesterday we started to learn how to identify author's purpose test talk. This will help us show what we know on the test. Let's activate our schema. Who remembers what we noticed about author's intent questions yesterday? Use the charts in the front to help you."

Nick looks at yesterday's chart and says, "We learned that there are two different kinds of questions about author's purpose. Some are about the purpose of the whole text, and some are about the purpose of a part, like a sentence or a word."

"Great! Yesterday you found test talk for both kinds of questions," Michelle says while gesturing toward the Test Talk for Author's Intent Questions chart on the board. "Now when you see test talk like that on the test, you'll know the test writers are asking you to find the author's purpose. Yesterday Kayla noticed something tricky about the answer choices of author's purpose questions. Does anyone remember what that was?"

"There was tricky test talk in the answer choices too—lots of it," Kiran says. "We need to make a chart about that, too."

"Good plan. I want you to find your partner from yesterday and a quiet place in the room to work. I'll pass out sample tests and sticky notes. Today I want you to hunt for the test talk in the answer choices of the author's purpose questions. When you find a tricky test talk word, write it down on a sticky, and we'll chart them during share time."

The students work for ten minutes while Michelle stops at each group to offer suggestions and ensure that both partners are participating. When the allotted time is over, she asks the students to bring their sticky notes to the carpet for share time. She calls on a few students at a time to come to the front of the room and put their sticky notes on a large piece of chart paper titled Test Talk for Author's Intent Answers.

When they finish collecting all of the test talk, the chart looks like this:

Answer Choices Test Talk

Explain	Tell about	Introduce
Teach	Persuade	Compare
Amuse	Entertain	Reveal
Prove	Tell readers how	Define
Give information	Frighten	Summarize
Give instructions	Convince	
Encourage the reader to…	Warn	
Express a concern	Show	
Advertise	Demonstrate	
Negotiate	Give an example	
Influence	Provide suspense	
Inquire	Make you laugh	
Point out	Show how to…	
Be humorous	Help understand	
Inform	Describe	

"Wow! We found *a lot* of test talk in those answer choices," Michelle says. "It looks like our test writers have a lot of different words to describe an author's purpose. I am looking at this list and thinking that it is a lot of words to remember. What do we usually do with a big list of words when we want to remember them or understand them better?"

The class answers in unison, "Sort them!" Michelle's class sorts words during word study, and it is one of their favorite activities.

"Great idea. Take a look at this list and talk to a partner about how you would sort them."

After a minute, Michelle asks who would like to share. Steven volunteers, "David and I decided to sort them by how many syllables they have. There are some with three syllables like *understand* and some with two like *describe*."

Michelle smiles and says, "That is good thinking, Steven. That would be a great sort for word study. I am wondering if that kind of sort would help us to organize and understand these words as test talk, though. Does anybody have a sort idea that has to do with the *meanings* of the words?"

Kayla raises her hand and says, "Todd and I noticed that lots of the words mean the same things, like *explain* and *teach*. Maybe we could sort them like that."

Michelle replies, "I love that idea! We know test talk is often just a bunch of tricky synonyms. I was thinking about how we learned to find the author's intent of a text. What do we do to find the purpose of a passage?"

"First we read the passage and look for clues to help us decide what type of text it is—like it could be a persuasive or instructional or informative text," Sarah offers. "There's one more I can't remember."

Jonathan calls out, "Entertaining text!"

Michelle moves the chart with the sticky notes to the side and puts a new chart on the board. It is also titled Test Talk for Author's Intent Answers, but this chart has four columns: Persuasive Texts, Instructional Texts, Informative Texts, and Entertaining Texts. "You know what I noticed about this huge list of test talk words? I think that each one of them goes with one of our text types. Jonathan, you remembered that *entertaining* is one type of text. Could you look at our test talk list and hunt for a test talk word that might be used to describe the purpose of an entertaining text?"

Jonathan asks, "Can I come up and get one?" Michelle nods, and Jonathan comes to the front, takes a sticky that reads "Make you laugh," and moves it to the Entertaining Text column of the new chart.

"Oh, I get it!" Ernesto calls out. "Can I do one?" "Sure," Michelle says, and Ernesto moves "Provide suspense" to the Entertaining Text column.

The sort continues, and when it is complete, Michelle says, "Now, the question of the day is this: how will knowing which test talk words go with which text types help you on the test? Talk to a partner for a minute and decide together." When Michelle asks for volunteers, all hands shoot into the air. Michelle calls on Jose.

"I think on the test we should do what we practiced in reading groups," he says. "We should read the passage and use the clues in the text to figure out what text type it is. Like if it has a lot of facts and dates, it might be an informative text. Then we can look at the answer choices and try to find test talk that goes with informative text. That will help us find the answer."

The other students nod in agreement. Michelle says, "Great! Remember though, that we found out today that some test talk goes with several different text types, so we have to read each answer completely and carefully. It's great to use our test talk knowledge and test-taking strategies, but what's the most important thing to use on the test?"

The class answers loudly, "Our brains!"

• • •   CONCEPT REVIEW LESSON

Target Question:
Do I remember how to identify the author's intent for writing a specific text?

Materials:
- Sample texts, one of each: entertaining, informative, persuasive, instructional
- Two-column chart titled Text Type/Author's Intent

Demonstration:

Begin by asking four students to role play the following situation: at the dinner table, three siblings are talking to their mother one at a time. Sibling One sings a silly song, Sibling Two begs her mom to get a puppy for the family, and Sibling Three tells her mom about the life cycle of the butterfly. While these students are rehearsing their roles, explain to the rest of the class that during the skit, the audience's job will be to decide what the purpose of each sibling's communication is.

After the skit, ask the audience for ideas about what each sibling's purpose was. Appropriate responses might be that Sibling One is trying to entertain, Sibling Two is trying to persuade, and Sibling Three is trying to inform. Refer to anchor charts from your Author's Intent unit to help the students activate their schema. Give students ample time to remember and discuss different purposes for communicating verbally.

Next, remind students that authors have an intent or purpose for writing, just as speakers have a purpose for talking. Finding the author's purpose is a skill that helps the reader understand a text more deeply. Ask students to discuss possible purposes for writing. Show and discuss a variety of text types including entertaining, informative, persuasive, and instructional texts. Lead think-alouds about the characteristics that help readers decide what type of text they're reading. For example, instructional texts may read like a manual or recipe, and may include diagrams. Remind students that after they identify a text type, it is easy to decide what the author's intent is; it's implied in the text type name. Sample text type ideas might be a silly poem, a magazine article, a personal letter, or a written complaint to a company.

Student Practice:

Ask students to hunt for a text in the classroom. Give them time to read their chosen text independently and think about the author's purpose for writing it. At the end of this independent reading time, ask students to partner up and share their text and ideas about the author's purpose.

Share:

Ask students to bring their texts to the carpet. Have volunteers share and record their ideas on a two-column chart, one column titled Text Type and the second Author's Intent. Encourage the students to use creative words to describe the author's purpose. For example, instead of saying "to persuade" repeatedly, try "to convince," "to cajole," or "to encourage." For homework, request that each student locate two more texts with different purposes and prepare to share them the following day.

Assess:

Notice students who need further instruction and reteach as needed before tomorrow's Test Talk lesson.

Further Steps:
- Take note cards into the hallway during bathroom breaks and play Name That Text Type games with the test talk words.
- Reteach during reading groups and individual reading conferences.
- Support this reading skill by teaching author's intent as a writing skill in writer's workshop. Give your student writers a particular purpose like "to persuade" and see what they come up with. The ability to transfer a concept to another area of study shows mastery.
- Have students share their writing with buddies and ask the buddy to guess what the author's purpose was for writing the text.

● ● ● **TEST TALK LESSON**

STRATEGY

Author's intent test talk

Target Question:
Can I find and understand author's intent test talk?

Materials:
- Test Talk for Author's Intent Questions and Test Talk for Author's Intent Answers anchor charts (If you have not created these charts with the class, prepare them for this lesson.)
- Signs that say Persuasive Text, Instructional Text, Entertaining Text, and Informative Text for the Four Corners game.
- Note cards labeled with each of the test talk words or phrases from the Test Talk for Author's Intent Answers anchor chart.
- Chart paper

Demonstration:

Remind students that the objective for these few lessons is to review what they learned during the year about author's intent in order to prepare for the test. Ask them to turn to a neighbor and complete the following two tasks: first, activate their schema by asking, "Hey brain, what do I know about finding the author's intent of a text?" Second, come up with a "kid talk" way to ask about author's intent. Kid talk is the opposite of test talk; it is casual, conversational language with which the kids are familiar. For example, an appropriate response might be, "Why did the author write this text, anyway?" After the partners have had a few minutes for discussion, allow them to share their ideas with the class.

Next, remind the students that the test's authors will use a completely different vocabulary than kids would when asking about author's intent. That vocabulary is called test talk. Refer students to the two anchor charts on the board and ask them to notice how these charts are different from the test talk charts from other units of study. Students will remember that there are two different test talk categories, one for the test questions, and one for the answers. They will also probably notice that there is a lot more test talk than usual on these charts. Remind students that while the list may seem overwhelming, it's not as scary as it looks because so many of the words or phrases mean exactly the same thing. The test authors use many different synonyms to describe the same author's purposes. This is why it's important to be able to translate these test talk synonyms and to know which text type they correspond to.

Use the chart to lead a think-aloud to model how students will use this process on the test. For example, "If you find an author's intent question about a passage, like the questions on Chart One, and you use the clues in the text and decide that that passage is an instructional text, what test talk words or phrases are likely to appear in the right answer choice?" Appropriate answers would include *show how to*, *explain how to*, *give instructions*, or *demonstrate*. Use the chart to discuss similar examples.

Student Practice:

Explain that today, students will get a chance to test their author's intent test talk knowledge by playing a game of team Four Corners. Divide students into teams of three. Place a text type sign in each of the four corners of the classroom and explain that you will call out and show a note card with a test talk answer word or phrase on it. Each team is to discuss and decide together which text type that test talk word or phrase might correspond to on the test. When they have made their decision, the entire team should move to the corner of their choice. After all the teams have chosen a corner, ask one student from each team to share why they made the decision they did. If the student can't explain it, the team is out for the next round. This rule involves all team members in the discussion and decision-making. Remind students that several of the test talk words correspond to different text types, so all teams don't need to end up in the same corner every round.

Share:
After the class has played using all of the test talk words and phrases, work together to create a new Test Talk for Author's Intent chart by tap-ing the note cards used in the game under the label for the corresponding text type. In cases in which the word or phrase might correspond to more than one text type, have students make more note cards.

Assess:
The teacher will gain insight through the discussions during Four Corners and share time about which students need further instruction.

• • •   PRACTICE WITH TEXTS LESSON

STRATEGY

Synthesizing author's intent con-tent, test talk, and test-taking strategies knowledge

Target Question:
Can I use my knowledge of author's intent, author's intent test talk, and test-taking strategies to successfully answer multiple-choice questions?

Materials:
- Transparency of demonstration passage and accompanying multiple-choice question
- Copies of student practice passages with multiple-choice questions
- Test Talk for Author's Intent anchor chart

Demonstration:

The teacher calls the class together to begin the focus lesson. She writes this question on the board: How do I find the author's intent of a text? She asks the students to think back to the past two lessons, turn to a buddy, and share responses. Students should respond with this process: read the text, find clues to decide what text type it is (informative, instructional, persuasive, or entertaining), and use this information to decide the author's intent. The teacher records this process on the board for later use during student practice, then asks the students, "What have you learned about author's intent test talk?" Student responses should include that test talk is different for questions and answers, that some questions ask about an entire text while others ask about parts of a text, and that most test talk corresponds to a particular text type.

The teacher tells the students that today they will put what they have learned about author's intent and test talk to the test—literally—by attempting to answer test-like multiple-choice questions. The teacher puts the demonstration passage and accompanying question on the overhead projector.

DEMONSTRATION PASSAGE:

In Australia, there are more than five thousand libraries. About seventy-two of those libraries are on wheels. Some mobile libraries cover the Gold Coast, a strip of beaches in the state of Queensland that runs north from the border with South Wales toward Brisbane, the state capital. Huge trucks and trailers carry thousands of books to children who cannot go to a library in a city. (Ruurs 2005)

What was the author's reason for writing this passage?

    A to prove that people should read more books
    B to entertain the reader by telling a humorous story
    C to give information about Australian geography
    D to inform the reader about different types of libraries in Australia

First, the teacher reads the question aloud and asks for volunteers to identify what test talk within the question leads the reader to believe it's about author's intent. Students will notice the test talk "author's reason for writing." The teacher then reads the passage twice to model rereading as a strategy, and begins a think-aloud about the clues in the text, circling them as they are identified, that lead her to the text type. For example, she might say, "These geographical locations and specific details lead me to believe that the author's purpose in this text was to inform." After the students have decided the passage is an informative text based on the clues, the teacher asks them to refer to the Informative Text column of the Test Talk for Author's Intent Answer chart to make predictions about what test talk the correct answer might contain. After students share their predictions, the teacher reads the question again and begins to consider each answer choice. She emphasizes the importance of reading each choice carefully and completely instead of using test talk as the only indicator of the correct choice. As demonstrated with choice C, sometimes test authors use the right test talk in the wrong answer choice to trick the test taker. Also, sometimes a question will have more than one good answer, but only one *best* answer. Remind students that while knowing test talk and strategies will help them succeed on the test, using their brains is the only way to avoid getting tricked.

The teacher asks the students to use what they know about author's intent, test talk, and test-taking strategies to help her find the best answer to the question. She reminds the students to use the Author's Intent anchor charts and the Test-Taking Strategies anchor chart as resources.

Student Practice:

The teacher pairs the students and tells them that now they will get a chance to practice finding the author's intent with a buddy. Each pair receives a student practice passage and the accompanying question. Students are to repeat the process modeled during demonstration. The teacher reminds them to use the Test Talk anchor charts and process chart as resources, and asks students to be prepared to explain the test talk they identified, the strategies they used to answer the question, and the thinking that led to their answer.

STUDENT PRACTICE PASSAGES:

Passage One

In 1887, the owners of all major league ball clubs agreed not to sign any more black players. Minor league owners followed suit. Determined to play professional ball, African Americans formed their own teams, beginning with the Cuban Giants in 1887. All-black teams prepared black players for the day that the major league would once again allow African Americans onto the field. (Weatherford 2005, 11)

In this passage, the author intended to

    A amuse the reader by telling an interesting story about baseball.

    B convince the reader that baseball is the best sport.

    C give information about the history of African Americans in baseball.

    D demonstrate how to become a great baseball player.

Passage Two
Geese
by Rudine Bishop (1999)

I saw some geese go strutting by
With heads and necks held very high.
I saw six geese upon the lawn,
And each had boots of orange on.

The poet probably included the phrase "boots of orange" to

    A compare the geese's feet to boots.

    B influence the reader to wear boots.

    C teach the reader about what geese wear.

    D prove that geese wear boots.

Passage Three
Dear Sarah,

Please come visit me at my new house! It is so fun here! I have lots of new friends, and if you come, I'll introduce you to them! Also, my mom said that if you get permission, she'll take us to the pool and maybe even to the movies! Ask your mom and call me if you can come. My new phone number is 455-6701. Hope to see you soon!

Love, Amanda

Amanda probably wrote this letter to

    A convince Sarah that Amanda's house was nicer than hers.
    B inform Sarah that she had a new phone number.
    C persuade Sarah to visit her.
    D describe her new friends to Sarah.

Passage Four

Dear Amanda,

My mom said that I can come over on Wednesday, but you need to pick me up. Here are the directions to my house.

- Start at the elementary school
- Take a left on Hidden Brook Street
- Take a right on Elm Street
- At the stop sign, turn left on Oak Court

My house is the 2nd brown house on the right. Remember, we have the funny purple mailbox. My address is 4701 Oak Court.

See you on Wednesday!

Sincerely, Sarah

The purpose of Sarah writing this passage was most likely to

    A warn Amanda that getting to her house was complicated.
    B show Amanda how to get to her house.
    C describe her house to Amanda.
    D make Amanda laugh by mentioning her purple mailbox.

Share:

After students have finished, the teacher asks them to gather and share their passages and answer choices with the class. Since each text type is represented, it is important that students get a chance to read and discuss all the passages. The teacher shows each passage with its question on the overhead as it is discussed. Groups can use the overhead to discuss their passage, circling the test talk and discussing the strategies they used. The teacher asks each group how the test authors tried to trick the students into choosing the wrong answers to their questions about author's intent. Students might notice that the test writers offer some choices that are good, but in each case only one answer is the best.

Assess:
Notice students who need further intervention.

Further Steps:
Have students practice this skill by trying to identify the intents of texts in their classroom, school, and community. For example, what is the intent of the class rules poster, the display of poems in the hallway, the posted information about the principal on a bulletin board, or a stop sign down the street?

Word study instruction is an area of uncertainty for many teachers; however, teaching students to understand, analyze, and spell words is a vital piece of a child's reading, writing, and speaking development. Historically, we have taught students about letters, sounds, and patterns in words and encouraged them to develop an ever-growing bank of known words. But meaning is also a significant piece of word study instruction, one that often appears on standardized tests.

Many standardized tests demand the ability to spell accurately, but they can also require the capability to analyze words, their parts, and their meanings. For example, students may be required to describe how a suffix changes the meaning of a word or to identify a word that has a particular prefix. In order to answer this type of question, students must know how words are built. They must be able to construct and deconstruct words with confidence, not just memorize how to spell them.

Learning how words are built directly parallels learning number sense in math. In the past, students memorized math facts as well as rules like "Write down the 1, carry the 10." As a result, students with strong memories passed tests, but they didn't necessarily understand numbers. When teachers started teaching real number sense, students began to learn how to manipulate, construct, and deconstruct numbers. This ability is what makes a mathematician. Understanding builds confidence, erasing the anxiety that can get in the way of learning new concepts.

This same principle can be applied to word study. Spelling words in the English language is much too complicated to learn solely by memorization and mnemonic devices. For many students, memorizing words every week does not help with reading or writing; memorizing words only prepares them to score well on Friday's test. Students must learn how to construct and deconstruct words and realize that understanding word parts will help them expand their reading and writing vocabulary as well as their spelling accuracy. If students understand how words work and know the language of word analysis questions, they will be able to answer them with confidence.

The next vignette illustrates careful, consistent word study instruction that is developmentally appropriate and assessment driven. This allows for children to meet the instruction at their level. The teacher does not follow a prescriptive guide with a given list of words. She relies on her knowledge of what each student needs to know and constantly assesses what her students need next. The students are not given spelling rules. Instead they discover, with teacher planning and guidance, what would be most useful to them as readers, writers, spellers, and speakers.

This lesson is designed to teach the formation of the past tense by adding the -*ed* suffix. The children in this classroom are not just learning to add the -*ed* suffix to the ends of words; they are also learning how adding the suffix changes the meaning. The teacher knows that this concept could appear on the reading SOL test in May, so she plans to connect this unit of study to word analysis questions as a way of preparing her students for the test. During these early lessons, she embeds vocabulary that she deems important to understanding test questions in this category without taking away from the instructional focus. At the end of the unit, she will teach direct lessons on the test talk for word analysis questions.

Beginning a Word Study Unit About the Suffix -*ed*

"Please come to the carpet for word study." It is noon in Lisa Antonelli's fourth-grade classroom, and she is ready to begin the daily word study block. Many of her students are in different stages of learning to speak English and, as a result, struggle with using the past tense in their reading, writing, and speaking. Some students don't use the past tense at all, while others try but are inconsistent because they don't fully understand it. She is beginning to teach a unit of study on the correct usage of the suffix -*ed* to form the past tense.

Using a transparency on the overhead projector, Lisa begins this unit with a shared reading of the poem "Ten Little Aliens" by Paul Janeczko. After reading the poem twice to enjoy it, Lisa asks, "Would someone like to come up and underline a word in the poem that is written to suggest that an action already happened?" Diego walks to the overhead projector and underlines *stayed*. Ten hands shoot into the air. Lisa calls on Joel, who walks to the overhead projector and underlines *climbed*. As each child underlines a word, Lisa writes it on a chart, recording the base or root word in red marker and the suffix -*ed* in blue marker.

Lisa is sure to use the terms *root* and *base* when she speaks, which helps the children be flexible in labeling the concept. She doesn't know which word might appear on the test and wants them to be ready for both.

After the underlining is complete, Lisa asks, "Could everyone please turn to a knee buddy and discuss what it is they think looks the same in all of the words?" As she moves around listening to each pair of children, she notes the buzz about the -*ed* at the end of each word. When the din subsides, Lisa asks, "Who wants to share?"

Cristain exclaims proudly, "There is an -*ed* at the end of each word."

Lisa responds, "That's right, Cristain. Adding the suffix -*ed* to a base or root word changes a word from present tense to past tense. Present tense means that something is happening right now and past tense means that it already happened." She explains further that -*ed* is a suffix, "just like -*ful*, which we studied back in October. It is a word part written at the end of a root or base word. It changes the word from present tense to past tense. Learning about suffixes like -*ed* and -*ful* will not only help you as a reader and a writer, but it will also help you analyze words on the SOL test."

Lisa specifically uses the term *suffix* because she knows it is likely to be on the SOL test. After she explains that -*ed* is a suffix like -*ful*, she holds up a large index card with the word *suffix* written on it. She knows that if students see *and* hear the term, they are more likely to be able to identify and use it to answer questions correctly on the test. When she finishes with the card, she places it back on the anchor chart entitled Word Study Test Talk, where she had put it during their study of the suffix -*ful*. This chart will be put into further use when the class studies the exact test language for word analysis questions.

Now Lisa looks at her students and says, "Please go back to your seat and collect words with the suffix -*ed* from your independent reading books." She hands the children a sticky note as they walk back to their tables. By collecting words from their own reading instead of being given a list, the students have more ownership over the task. They also become accustomed to reading -*ed* words in context, which is what they will have to do on the test. After about ten minutes the students come back up to the carpet and share their new -*ed* words. Lisa adds them to the class list, and the class rereads the list.

The next day, Lisa starts the word study block by asking her students to examine the list, notice the base or root word, and note how it changes when -*ed* is added. She gives them time to reread the list and note the changes in the base or root word. While they are thinking, Lisa watches the class intently and jots down anecdotal notes about who seems actively or passively on-task and who seems actively or passively off-task. These notes will inform her choices about seating during whole-class lessons. "Boys and girls, please turn to a knee buddy and discuss what you noticed."

Khadra talks to Jennifer. "When you make *jump* into *jumped*, you just add -*ed*; the *jump* part stays the same."

Jennifer nods and declares, "When you change *shop* into *shopped*, you put two *p*'s in the middle." Lisa moves around, taking notes on what the children say to their partners. She is looking to see who is grasping the concept that the base word can change when you add -*ed* and who will need more assistance or small-group instruction.

When they are done speaking to their knee buddies, Lisa asks Khadra and Jennifer to share what they talked about. As they explain *jump* and *jumped*, Lisa writes the two words on the whiteboard. "I would like you to organize these words based on how the base word changes when you add -*ed*," she says. "You will find more than one category." Lisa is specific about how she wants the words sorted. She knows that if she suggests an open sort, some students might sort by the first letter of the alphabet or the vowel sounds. Although an open sort is productive for some word study principles, today it would dilute what she wants the children to learn.

She organizes the children into groups of four or five and sends each group off with a copy of the class -*ed* list and their word study notebooks. Sorting is not new to the students, so Khadra and Jennifer's example should be enough to get them started. As the groups settle in, Lisa notes that the children naturally scoot together into pairs and discuss the list. Lisa walks over to observe Sara and Oliver. Sara says, "Hey Oliver, I think *rotted* and *shopped* go together because the consonant at the end of the base word is written twice before the -*ed*." Oliver agrees and then says, "Let's write *carried* and *copied* in a list together because the *y* at the end of the base word is taken away and then you write -*ied*." Lisa continues to walk around with her clipboard and record how each group or pair works together and what the students are noticing about -*ed* words.

After the students have been working for about fifteen minutes, Lisa asks them to finish and come back to the carpet. She asks each group to share one category of -*ed* words that they found and two words that fit that category. As each group shares, Lisa records the title of a category, and two words that fit in it, on three different index cards. She places the index cards together in a pocket chart. When Cindy shares, she says, "I think *jumped* and *jammed* go in the same category because they both begin with *j*."

Lisa quickly responds, "Cindy, I notice you sorted those two words by the beginning letter. Do you think that will help you know what happens to the base word when you add -*ed*?" Cindy is stumped for a moment and then her face lights up. She exclaims, "Maybe *jammed* goes in the list with *hopped* and *skipped* because you add an extra *m* at the end of the base word."

Lisa then asks Cindy, "Does *jumped* go in the same list?"

"Hmmmm," murmurs Cindy. "No, because it doesn't have two *p*'s."

"I'll put it over here, and we can see if it matches another category that someone shares." Lisa places the index card with *jumped* in the corner of her pocket chart for the time being.

After the children have shared the categories compiled during small-group work, Lisa asks them to take some time and reread the lists in the pocket chart. Next she tells them to think about what they know or notice about what happens to the base word when you add -*ed* to make the word past tense. She gives about two or three minutes to reread and think. Then she hands out sticky notes and pencils and asks them to quickly jot down any generalizations that they noticed. When the students are done, they save the sticky note in their word study notebooks. Then Lisa says, "Tomorrow's lesson will begin with a discussion of what you wrote on your sticky notes. Be ready to share."

This window into the launch of Lisa's unit on -*ed* highlights how she explicitly teaches her students about the suffix while at the same time the children are taking ownership of their learning. With her support, they are discovering how to use -*ed* and how it changes the meaning of a word. She hopes that when this unit is complete, her students will be competent using the past tense in their reading, writing, and speaking. She knows some students will continue to need instruction with this concept.

Even in these first few days of the unit, Lisa uses specific vocabulary that will prime her students for the vocabulary on the test. In planning the unit, she has considered what the students need to know for the test but has also been careful not to overdo talk of the test right now. First and foremost, she wants the skill to be useful to her students as readers, writers, and speakers.

Wrapping It Up: Test Talk Lesson

The students in Lisa's class are completing the unit of study on the suffix -*ed*. During the last two days of the unit, she plans to expose the children to the language of the test questions that ask about suffixes. She searches through released test items from the past few years to find common language that will help them transfer their newly acquired knowledge of suffixes to test questions on the same topic. Normally, at the end of a broader unit like the one on main idea, she would ask the children to search through released items to find the appropriate kinds of test questions themselves. However, because this is a very specific unit within ongoing word study, Lisa has dispensed with her usual practice in order to center the students' attention on suffix test talk.

She starts the lesson by putting a sample test passage, entitled "Birds in Flight," on the overhead for shared reading. Lisa reads the title and asks the students to take a minute to think and activate their schema about the title. She chooses not to ask the students to share their thoughts with a knee buddy because they won't be able to do this on the test. Activating their schema, or thinking about what they already know about the title, is a known reading strategy for all of them. The whole school uses this particular language, so her students know exactly what to do and why they are doing it.

Asking her students to activate their schema at the beginning of this test talk lesson may seem to have nothing to do with word study, but Lisa believes it is imperative to integrate all useful strategies for success on the test, even when she is teaching for something specific.

Lisa waits while the children think in silence about what they know about the text, based on the title. After thirty seconds she begins a shared reading of the text from the released item. After reading the text, Lisa identifies one question under the passage that she wants the students to examine and answer. The word used in the question, *lovely*, is included in the text. Although the released items include a few types of word analysis questions, she finds an example that includes suffixes. She wants the students to connect what they learned about suffixes in the unit to how the test will ask them about the concept. Lisa knows the test questions will use language that is different from her instruction. If her students don't understand the language of the question, they may get the answer wrong, even if they understand and are flexible with the concept.

The class reads the question with Lisa.

In which word does *-ly* mean the same as it does in *lovely*?

A casually
B lye
C analyze
D lying

She stops at the end of the question and asks, "Is there anything you know or are sure about in this question?"

Silvia raises her hand. "The *-ly* in *lovely* is underlined. That is a clue that it is important."

Oliver says, "The *-ly* is at the end of a word, so I think it is a suffix."

"How can you be sure it is a suffix, Oliver?" Lisa asks. Oliver is silent.

Jose speaks up. "If you take *-ly* away from the base word *love*, then you still have a whole word, so *-ly* is a suffix."

"That's right, Jose. *-Ly* on the end of *lovely* is a suffix, just like *-ful* and *-ed*. So far, we know that the word *lovely* has the *-ly* suffix. What else do you know?"

Cindy pipes up. "Well, the question has *means the same* in it. In math, that is like *equal to* or *the same as*."

"What do you think this question is asking you to do?" asks Lisa.

"I think this question is asking which word uses *-ly* as a suffix, instead of just as a regular part of the word."

"Terrific, Cindy," says Lisa. "Now we know that questions about suffixes that say, 'In which word does a suffix mean the same as it does in another word?' are asking us to choose which answer uses the suffix in the same way. So, for example, in the question we looked at, *lovely* used *-ly* as a suffix, and we needed to choose another word that did the same thing."

The students read through the answers together and eliminate the second, third, and fourth answers. Many suggest that none of the last three answers can be correct because *-ly* isn't even at the end of the word, much less a suffix. Juan Carlos said, "I think it is *casually*. It's the best answer because *casual* is the root word and *-ly* is the suffix. None of the other choices have *-ly* at the end, so they aren't a suffix."

"Thanks, Juan Carlos," says Lisa. She quickly writes the wording for this question on a sentence strip, reads it to the class, and places it on the Reading Test Talk anchor chart, where a collection of sentence strips is gathering.

The next day, Lisa teaches one more test talk lesson related to suffixes and reviews test talk for word analysis questions. She will return to word analysis questions at the end of her next word study unit, using a sample question or two that match the principle being studied. Then she plans to revisit word analysis questions during the review unit shortly before the test. By doing this kind of lesson attached to the end of a unit of study, the students are able to connect what they learn in such a way that it makes them better readers, writers, spellers, and test takers. It is time well spent, not just disconnected test-prep time.

CONCEPT REVIEW LESSON   • • •

Target Question:
Do I remember how word parts help me spell and understand the meaning of a word?

STRATEGY

Analyzing words and their parts

Materials:
- Individual student whiteboards
- Dry erase markers
- Erasers

- Sticky notes
- Independent reading book

Demonstration:

The teacher writes the following number on the board: $50.02. She asks the students how they would read the number. Then she writes $500.02 on the board and asks the students what is the same and what is different in these two numbers. She asks how the location of the decimal within these digits affects the value (meaning) of the number. She suggests that the location of the decimal determines the meaning of the number, similar to the way a prefix or suffix determines the meaning of a word.

Next, the teacher writes the root word *read* on the board. Then she writes *reread* and asks her students what is the same and what is different in the two words. She asks how the prefix affects the root word. She then writes other root words on the board, such as *connect*, *jump*, *usual*, and *plow*. She asks the students to add prefixes and/or suffixes, to consider the meaning of the prefix and/or suffix, and then to consider how this changes the meaning of the root word. She explains that knowing the meaning of the parts of the word will help students spell the word.

Student Practice:

The teacher asks the students to go back to their seats and read a book to find words with prefixes and/or suffixes and to record them on sticky notes. After seven to ten minutes, the teacher asks the students to compare their lists with a partner and then borrow any words from their partner's list to add to their own (share, compare, borrow).

Then the teacher asks each pair to choose one word from their two lists, write it on a sticky note, and put it in a box at the front of the room. She picks a few words and asks for volunteers to play Charades with the class. First, each volunteer will act out the root word. The second time, the child will act out the same word with the prefix or suffix included. The teacher should model this before the class begins the game.

Share:

The teacher asks each pair to share one word from their list (a different word from the one they picked for Charades) and explain the meaning of the root word, how the word meaning changes when the prefix and/or suffix is added, and how knowing the meaning of the parts of words enables them to spell the word.

Assess:
The teacher notices students who need further intervention.

Further Steps:
- Collect words around the school (hallways, office, etc.) that contain prefixes and/or suffixes. Ask students to explain the meaning of the root word, how the word meaning changes when the prefix and/or suffix is added, and how knowing the meaning of the parts of the words enables them to spell the word.
- As students return to their seats from the gather space, ask them to name a word and then change it by using a prefix or suffix.

TEST TALK LESSON   • • •

Unlike the more specific lesson on suffixes above, this lesson includes all possible test talk for word analysis type questions.

STRATEGY

Identifying word study test talk and understanding its meaning

Target Question:
Can I find and understand word study test talk?

Materials:
- Word Study Test Talk anchor chart
- Practice test passage and questions transparency
- Student copy of test passage and questions
- Labels for Four Corners game

Demonstration:
The teacher hangs up the Word Study Test Talk anchor chart, which includes questions like:

In paragraph two, the word ... means ...
In which word does *re-* mean the same as in *reread*?
Which word is the root word for ... ?

The teacher reminds students that they are reviewing the idea that adding or changing word parts changes the meaning of a word. Today they will practice identifying word study test talk and understanding its meaning. Then the teacher might ask students to predict which words, phrases, and questions they might notice in word study test talk. Students may suggest answers such as: *root word*, *means*, *in paragraph four*, *prefix*, *means the same as*, etc. The students can use the Word Study Test Talk anchor chart for support.

Next, the teacher demonstrates slow, careful reading and rereading of the directions, test passage, test questions, and answer choices. As the teacher notices test talk, she circles it and discusses how she knows that it is a word study question. Last, she discusses the meaning of the test talk included in the question.

The teacher also thinks aloud about any test-taking strategies that support answering this type of question. Give the students time to observe, discuss, and question. The teacher and students may refer to the established test talk anchor chart to review the meaning of word study phrases and questions.

Student Practice: Four Corners Game

The teacher informs the students that they will play Four Corners, a game to help them practice identifying word study test talk and reinforce its meaning. If the game has not been played before, teacher should model. Each corner of the room will symbolize a different kind of test question. One corner will be word analysis; the next corner could be poetry; another, author's intent; and another, character traits (or whatever the teacher chooses). The corners could also be specific word analysis categories: a prefix corner, a contraction corner, etc. The teacher might choose to label the corners.

The teacher reads test talk words, phrases, and questions from test talk anchor charts, one at a time. After the children listen to the teacher read the test talk, each child will decide which category that particular test talk matches. Each child must then walk over to the corner that matches that category and stand. The teacher then asks the students (no matter what corner they have chosen) to talk to the person next to them about which words helped them know that particular test talk belongs to the type of question they have chosen. Some students may choose to move to a different corner once they discuss the language with a friend. When the students have chosen the word study corner, ask them to discuss the meaning of the test talk in the given question. The teacher can listen in on the discussion and take notes on student progress. Continue discussion and questions until everyone understands the concept.

Share:

The teacher asks the students to share what they already knew about word study test talk (or a specific category) before they started Four Corners, and what was something new they learned or thought about.

Assess:

Take note of which students consistently struggle with choosing the right corner and continue test talk practice in small groups.

PRACTICE WITH TEXT LESSON • • •

Target Question:

Can I use my knowledge about words, word study test talk, and test-taking strategies to answer multiple-choice questions?

Materials:

- "Azerbaijan" text transparency
- *Dream Makers* transparency
- *Dream Makers* student copy
- Test Talk anchor chart
- Test-Taking Strategies chart

STRATEGY

Synthesizing content, test talk, and test-taking strategy knowledge

Demonstration:

The teacher tells students that today is the big day. Today they will use their word study knowledge, their test talk knowledge, and test-taking strategies to practice answering word study questions. She starts by asking the following questions, one at a time: What do you know about words and their meanings? What test talk do you know for word study questions? What strategies might you use when answering these questions? The teacher places the "Azerbaijan" text on the overhead projector.

DEMONSTRATION PASSAGE:

From *My Librarian Is a Camel: How Books Are Brought to Children Around the World* (Ruurs 2005)

Directions: Read the passage and answer the questions that follow.

Azerbaijan

The children in the Kelenterli refugee settlement can't sit still when they know that the blue truck is coming! The blue library truck is here, thanks to the hard work of Relief International, an organization that provides relief to victims of natural disasters and civil conflicts.

These children live in poverty, but the blue library truck brings a surge of happiness and curiosity. "It's a big event when the library comes to town," says the librarian. "It's a bit of happiness for children who normally don't have much to look forward to."

1. In which word does *-ment* mean the same as it does in the word *settlement*?

   A lament
   B mentor
   C mention
   D judgment

2. Which word contains a root word?

   A poverty
   B happiness
   C don't
   D library

The teacher thinks aloud. "The first thing I notice is the directions. I need to read them and underline the verbs. I need to *read* and *answer*." Next, the teacher reads the passage. "Hmmm... I'm not sure I understood the whole passage. I think I will reread it." Next, as the teacher reads the test questions, she circles the test talk. "I know how to take words apart, but do I know how to answer this question?" Then she discusses the meaning of the test talk in each question. "Well, *-ment* is a suffix, so I need to figure out which of these answer choices also uses *-ment* as a suffix and not just part of the word."

The teacher continues to model understanding of test talk and knowledge of content to answer the questions. Seamlessly, the teacher also models test-taking strategies she would use to answer the questions. "Let me see, in number 2 I need to eliminate which answer choices don't have root words. Well, *poverty* has no word that stands on its own. *Povert* is not a word. So that can't be the answer..." Once the teacher has thoroughly modeled her thinking process with the demonstration poem and two questions provided, the students should be ready to work independently.

Student Practice:

The teacher hands out the following practice sheet to individual children, partners, or small groups. She asks the children to complete the practice sheet and be ready to explain why they chose their answers. They should also be ready to share the strategies they used and how they knew what the test talk was asking them to do.

STUDENT PRACTICE PASSAGE:

From *Dream Makers: Young People Share Their Hopes and Aspirations* (Waldman 2003)

Directions: Read the poem and answer the questions that follow.

I VisualizeMyself
by Jane Yang (2003)

I visualize myself
in a world full of possibilities,
a place where all my dreams
become reality

I imagine myself
in an environment where I can

make a difference,
alert for upcoming surprises

I can picture myself
keeping the world growing
for future generations,
facing many challenges
and unlocking the unknown

1. In which word does *un-* mean the same as in *unlocking*?

    A unbelievable

    B United States

    C begun

    D unique

2. In the third stanza, the word *unknown* means

    A knowing many things.

    B not known.

    C intelligent.

    D familiar.

Share:

Students should explain why they chose their answers, what strategies they used, and how they knew what the test talk was asking them to do.

Assess:

Teacher notices students who need further intervention.

Further Steps:

Students can write word study test questions and then explain them to the class. After the student-generated questions are approved by the class, they can be placed in a hat. Then the class can invite guest test takers to come to the classroom and pick a question out of the hat. The students then coach the guest test taker about how to use content knowledge, test talk, and test-taking strategies to answer the questions.

In her book *Awakening the Heart: Exploring Poetry in Elementary and Middle School*, Georgia Heard (1999) quotes Roque Dalton: "Poetry, like bread, is for everyone" (xvii). Poetry offers language structure, vocabulary, rhythms, images, comfort, insights—and, not least, pleasures—that we may never be exposed to in prose. Anyone who has read a poetry book to a young child learns to pause at the end of each verse to allow the young listener the opportunity to supply the rhyming conclusion, which the child awaits with an almost proprietary sense of anticipation. Children are enthralled by the simplicity and power of Blake's "Tyger! Tyger! burning bright." They delight in memorizing these lines, which give voice to their own intense experience of nature's terror and beauty. They can intuit that Wordsworth's "My heart leaps up when I behold / A rainbow in the sky" is fundamentally different from the meteorologist's "50 percent chance of showers, but then expect afternoon sunshine." Poetry is for children, as for the rest of us, that "spontaneous overflow of powerful feelings" that Wordsworth so aptly described.

Teachers appreciate the numerous benefits of poetry for their students, insisting on time for poetry in their classrooms as a matter of habit. Some teach a poetry workshop once a week, while others teach a long unit of study once a year. Still others read poetry daily and use poems as mentor texts during reading and writing workshop.

Whatever the mode of presentation, teachers are eager for their students to feel comfortable with poetry, to be as familiar with the poetry shelves at the library as the fantasy shelves, to regard Langston Hughes as they do J. K. Rowling. As educators, we want poetry to reach the heart, soul, and mind of our most struggling students, allowing them a feeling of success. Often, students who are challenged by reading and writing lengthy prose can read a poem instead and gain greater understanding of themselves and the world around them. With the infusion of high-stakes testing, however, this goal may be an elusive one. Poetry for the sake of enjoyment, enrichment, and expression is in danger of being squeezed out in the name of test-driven poetry instruction.

The point is driven home in the movie *Dead Poets Society* (Weir 1989), in which the inspirational English teacher John Keating suggests that the standard method of teaching poetry simply will not do. He invites his pupils to tear out the introduction of their poetry textbook, because it suggests that one's enjoyment of poetry grows through graphing and rating meter, rhyme, and patterns of speech. Dramatically he proclaims, "This is a battle, a war, and the casualties could be your hearts and souls." He encourages his students to seize the joy of language, to live life to the fullest, to read and write poetry in order to be part of the human race. We propose that, as teachers, we can do both: we can satisfy the test requirement without giving up the delights and intellectual rigor of poetry.

Standardized tests frequently include poetry, demanding that students be able to identify the conventions of poetry, such as stanza or rhyme scheme, or be able to interpret a poem for meaning. Before diving into the business of testing on poetry, teachers must first lure their students into the magic and thrill of poetry for its own sake. Reading poetry to, with, and by students, discussing poets and poems, and having students compose their own poems are prerequisites to making sure that students learn how to answer poetry questions in a testing situation. Thus, poetry can be taught as an art *and* a science.

Teachers can attend to the joy of poetry while including the skills needed to understand and answer poetry questions on a test. To omit poetry from students' literacy instruction would leave a monumental gap in their literary, intellectual, and emotional development.

First Lesson in Year-Long Poetry Workshop

Georgia Heard says, "Every writer of poetry is first a reader of poetry" (1989, 1). The following classroom vignette demonstrates the beginning of the study of poetry in a fifth-grade classroom. In this lesson, the choral reading of poems begins to immerse students in poetry while leveling the playing field for all readers. The enjoyment and playfulness of the activity draws in the whole class, not just the students who already enjoy poetry.

Even in this early lesson, the teacher carefully drops in poetry vocabulary, but she is not heavy-handed with test prep. The purpose of the lesson, or a series of lessons, is to draw students in and to begin to build interest in poetry. It should be fun, fun, fun.

In this particular classroom, two teachers team teach during the language arts block. All children are included; no one leaves the room for a special class or to see a special teacher. These two teachers, in this case the classroom teacher and a reading teacher, plan together once a week and share responsibility for instruction. Sometimes they teach the mini-lessons together. Sometimes one will have the major responsibility for the lesson while the other takes copious notes on the children's comments, questions, and behaviors during the lesson. Both teachers review the notes during planning sessions and use them to inform their instruction.

"Come gather 'round the overhead; it's time for poetry workshop. The action is on the screen." Amy is team teaching in Jennifer Orr's fifth-grade classroom, and this is her lesson to teach. Jen will take notes on the children and may jump in to expand on something Amy or one of the students has said. Most likely, Jen will teach the next lesson while Amy takes notes. Amy points out that the action is on the screen so that the children will know where to turn their attention, as sometimes they work from an easel or a read-aloud in the teacher's hands.

"Today we are going to begin poetry workshop, and it will continue every Monday for the rest of the year," Amy says. Some students smile with delight, while others look a little puzzled and a few look downright gloomy. Amy puts a transparency with a poem on the overhead projector. "I want to share a few of my favorite poems with you," she says. "After I share them, we are going to have some fun reading them together." She notes that Oscar's frown changes slightly.

Amy reads the poem "Big" by Colin McNaughton (1994), a poem that includes synonyms for the word *big*. She waits several seconds and then reads it again. "I always like to read poems at least twice," she says. "It helps me really hear the words and think about the poem more deeply. Now, let's have some fun with 'Big.' We'll start with whisper voices and then get a little louder with each word. By the end, we should be using really loud voices, but not so loud that Ms. Byram's class can hear us through the walls." The children begin to read very quietly and slowly get louder. The energy in the room picks up, and the body language of many students begins to change. By the end, all the students are reading loudly and there is an undertone of giggling, but everyone is still actively on-task.

When the reading is done, David asks, "Can we do it again?"

"Sure. This time, let's do the opposite. We can start loud and get quieter." The students are delighted.

Next, Amy puts "Poem," a serious poem by Langston Hughes (1994) about losing a friend, on the overhead projector. She reads the poem twice. Then she asks the students to read it with her. Without prompting, the students read "Poem" in a somber tone. Amy asks, "Why did you read this poem so differently from 'Big'?"

Samantha says, "It's sad."

"Tell me more."

"Well," Samantha says, "It's like the poet's best friend moved away or something."

Celeste suggests, "Maybe the friend died. If someone died, you don't want to read the poem in a happy, fun way. It makes you feel sad, so you read sad."

"Read sad? What do you mean?" Amy asks.

"You read it quietly, like you would talk if someone was telling you about something sad in their life."

"Interesting, Celeste," says Amy. "Would anyone like to suggest a way the whole class should read it?" she asks.

Mohammed speaks up. "Let's read it so the boys read the first line and then the girls read the next line. We'll alternate."

"Sounds good." The students read the poem; all are engrossed, yet solemn.

Viviana says, "Let's do it again, with the girls starting and the boys reading the second line."

"OK," Amy says.

After the class reads "Poem" several times, Amy suggests that it has just one stanza. "A stanza is one of the ways a poet divides up a poem. A poem can have one stanza or many, many stanzas." Amy writes the word *stanza* on a sentence strip and asks Tom to tape it up on the poetry anchor chart, which will eventually be titled Poetry Conventions. If this lesson came later in the class study of poetry, she might dwell more on the definition of the word *stanza*. This is just the beginning, so she wants to hook the kids on poetry before she gets into technical vocabulary.

Amy places a transparency of "Harriet Tubman" by Eloise Greenfield (1978) on the overhead and reads it twice, emphasizing powerful words and reading certain parts with attitude. Amy asks the students, "Any suggestions for how to read this poem together?"

After a bit of silence, Gabriel raises his hand. "I think we should stand up and do hand gestures."

Amy asks, "What comes to mind?"

"Well, maybe during the first part we should shake our fingers, like we are trying to make a point."

"That sounds terrific, but what do you mean by the first part?" asks Amy.

"I mean the part that starts with the words *Harriet Tubman* and ends with *stay one either*."

Amy points to the first stanza on the screen. "Oh, you mean this part? This is the first stanza of the poem. Gabriel, how did you recognize it was a particular 'part' of the poem?"

"Well, there is a space after the last sentence of that part."

"Oh, what you are thinking of as a sentence is called a line in poetry. It's a little different than a sentence. But you are on to something really important. You can tell a stanza is over because there is white space between the end of the last line and the beginning of the first line in the next stanza. Thanks, Gabriel. By the way, since he brought it up, I will add the word *line* to our poetry chart." Amy knows that the words *stanza* and *line* are important vocabulary for the children to know for the test. She will revisit the concepts in full as students get deeper into their study of poetry.

Gabriel suggests a few other gestures and movements to use during their reading of "Harriet Tubman." He thinks students should wave a hand when they read the word *Farewell!* and run softly in place beginning with the line "Ran looking for her freedom" and ending with the last line of the next stanza. The ending will include more finger shaking and a whisper reading of the last line, like an echo. As the students read it, their sense of "attitude" grows along with their enjoyment of reading poetry.

Jen Orr, the classroom teacher, has been sitting with the kids on the floor, taking notes and reading poetry along with the rest of the group. Although she is not outwardly involved in this particular lesson, her role is crucial. She has noted the comments of the students who are actively involved and the body language of the rest of the group. She is watching particular students who are often actively or passively off-task, redirecting them when necessary. She is noticing that some students who often sit in the back of the gather area are scooting forward, slowly but surely. This poetry is for them, too.

The next Monday, Jen repeats the same style of lesson, sharing a few poems and engaging the students in reading them many different ways. Amy takes notes while sitting on the floor with the students. When the two teachers meet later in the week, they discuss their notes and use them to plan their next poetry workshop. They are pleased with student engagement and feel they are beginning to hook the class on poetry. Their next lessons will continue to include whole-class poetry reading but will go beyond just a suggestion of poetry conventions. They will dive deeper into terms like *line*, *stanza*, *white space*, and *rhyme scheme* as well as poets' decision-making when using these conventions. Their goal is to expose their students to the joy and rigor of poetry while subtly preparing them for testing—which is also for everyone.

Wrapping It Up: Test Talk Lesson

Having enjoyed the rich work of poetry workshop this year, the students in Jennifer Orr's class are approaching test time. They have read myriad poems aloud and silently, discussed them in small and large groups, learned many conventions of poetry, collected poems for personal anthologies, written reflections, written their own poetry to share with peers, teachers, and parents, and participated in a poetry slam. Each week, poetry workshop has been greeted with hushed cheers; missing it for a band concert or school play brought huge disappointment. Poetry is for everyone in Jen's class.

In team planning sessions, Amy, Jen, and other members of the fifth-grade team have been perusing released items from the state to gather language used in poetry test questions. This language includes words, phrases, full sentences, and questions. They know their students have been taught the poetry concepts required by the state but want to make sure the students look as "poetry smart" on the test as they really are.

As the class begins poetry workshop. Jen explains that since the state test is getting closer, poetry workshop will seem a little different today. "Let's begin by reading our poetry conventions chart," she says. The students read the words and phrases they have collected all year as they were taught how to read and write poetry. Then she asks each child to turn to a buddy and talk about what they learned about reading and writing poetry in poetry workshop this year. Next, she asks the students to form partnerships and for one person from each pair to pick up a packet. The packets include all kinds of test passages and questions, not just poetry. She asks the students to use highlighters to mark the poetry questions as they read through the passages, poems, and questions in their packets. She wants to make sure they talk it out with their partners and are ready to explain how they know the question they highlighted is a poetry question. "Go ahead and get started. Ms. Greene and I will visit each partnership to see how it's going. You will have about ten minutes."

As the two teachers walk around the classroom, they notice students reading and talking to each other about each question. Some students are glancing at the Poetry Conventions chart on the wall, and others are using their personal copies as a way to confirm their findings. Jen listens to Viviana and Samantha. Samantha says, "I think that some of the passages are long narratives, some are nonfiction, like the one about turtles, and some are poems. The poetry questions will always be after poems! So let's not pay as much attention to the questions after the narratives and non-fiction texts." The girls look at Jen, and she says, "Girls, that is a very important point. Please make sure you share that with the class."

Jen moves on to Ngan and Gabriel, who are rereading a question in their sample packet. As they read, they look back and forth between the question and Ngan's personal poetry conventions list. Ngan says, "This must be a poetry question because it has the word *stanza* in it." Jen smiles and moves on.

After ten minutes, Jen calls the class back to share circle. She asks, "What did you find?" The kids look at one another for a minute and then Samantha's hand shoots up. Jen is glad the class will get to hear her important point first.

"After looking at the passages," says Samantha, "my partner and I noticed that there is a difference in how they look. The narratives and nonfiction passages are long, with sentences and paragraphs. The poems are shorter, and have lines, stanzas, and white space. There will only be poetry questions after the poems."

"Would anyone like to add on to Samantha's thought?" asks Jen.

Gabriel says, "My partner and I noticed that, too. We kind of stopped reading the narratives and nonfiction texts and went right to the poems. It was easy to know what to highlight after we did that."

Gabriel's partner Ngan speaks up. "I used my poetry conventions chart to check some of the words in the poetry questions, just to be sure. I noticed words like *stanza* and *line*. But I also noticed something different in the poem. Each poem had numbers next to each line, and then some of the questions said, 'In line nine . . . .' I think the test writers wanted to make it a little easier so we don't have to count to line nine to be able to answer the question."

"I think you've got something there," says Jen.

While Jen listens to the students, Amy has placed a blank chart labeled Poetry Test Talk next to the Poetry Conventions chart. Jen asks, "So who can tell us about a poetry question you located?"

Christina raises her hand. "Here's one. 'What feeling does the speaker show in line two?'"

"How do you know that is a poetry question, Christina?" asks Jen.

"Well, like Samantha said, there is a poem just before the question, and the question has the word *line* in it. It also asks about the speaker, which is on our chart from a few months ago."

"So, what should we put on the Poetry Test Talk chart?" asks Jen. "How about, 'What feeling does the speaker show . . . .'" Amy records this on the chart in red marker. The whole Poetry Test Talk chart will be in red. Choosing just one color makes it easier for the brain to remember and use the information on the chart later. After Amy writes the question on the chart, she asks the students to reread it. Amy and Jen know that they want the students to *see* and *hear* the language of the test, the better to remember and understand it on test day. Jen asks, "Christina, what do you think the test authors are really asking?"

"Well, the speaker means who is talking in the poem, so it is asking how the speaker feels in a particular part of the poem—like if the speaker is sad or mad or something."

"Great. Any questions?" asks Jen.

"I'm not sure about the speaker of the poem," David says.

"Can someone explain the speaker of the poem to David?"

Celina raises her hand. "I think I can explain it. It's like the narrator or who is talking in the poem."

Amy jumps in. "I want to add on to Celina's wise words. I would like to remind you that the speaker often doesn't tell you how she is feeling; you have to infer it. You will have to reread the poem many times, think about what you know, and put it together with the words in the poem. You will have to infer. David, have we helped you?"

"Yep, I get it now," says David.

Jen says, "Let's add one more question to our chart today. What other kinds of poetry questions did you notice?"

Heather says, "There is a question about rhyme scheme. It says, 'Which rhyme scheme is used in this poem?'"

"Hmmm...what does that mean?" Jen asks.

"I think it's asking about the rhyme pattern at the end of each line, like *aabb* or *abca*. It's on our Poetry Conventions chart from when we worked on it earlier in the year," Heather says.

Jen asks, "What should Ms. Greene write on the test talk chart?"

"How about 'Which rhyme scheme is used?'" Heather suggests.

"Great," exclaims Jen. "Any questions about rhyme scheme?" The class is quiet, and a few students are shaking their heads. "Let's put these packets away and come back to this tomorrow." The students continue to work on developing the Poetry Test Talk chart during reading workshop the next day. They need more time than the usual weekly poetry workshop, as test time is approaching.

Though this lesson and others like it may seem dry compared to the richness of the weekly poetry workshop, the students are interested and engaged. They are thinking and discovering test talk themselves, instead of just being handed a list of types of poetry questions. They are interested in the challenge of test talk. It is a routine they have become accustomed to, it doesn't take a lot of time, and they know that it will help them feel more confident on the day of the test.

● ● ●   **CONCEPT REVIEW LESSON**

STRATEGY

Identify and understand conventions of poetry

Target Question
Do I remember and understand the conventions of poetry?

Materials:
- Transparency of poem
- Blank chart paper

- Packet of poetry for student practice (or poems from their poetry anthology or poetry folders)
- Highlighter
- Poetry Conventions anchor chart

Demonstration:

The teacher asks the students to think about the last time they went to a swimming pool. What are the "conventions" of a swimming pool? (They should be familiar with the term *conventions* or whatever term is applicable.) The students might say that there is a lifeguard, clear water, a shallow end and a deep end, a diving board, etc. The teacher records the conventions of a swimming pool on a piece of chart paper. Next, she explains that these conventions are what make a swimming pool a swimming pool, not a lake or the ocean.

With the class Poetry Conventions anchor chart in full view, the teacher places a transparency of a poem on the overhead projector. She reminds the students that poets use many conventions when writing a poem. She reads the poem twice and then, as she reads it a third time, she thinks aloud about what conventions she notices. She may suggest terms like *white space, lines, line breaks, stanzas, similes, rhyme scheme* (if the poem rhymes), *rhythm, free verse*, etc. She reminds students that these conventions are what makes a poem poetry, not prose.

Student Practice:

The teacher asks the students to form groups of four. Each group is given two copies of the poetry packet, and the students are asked to mark and list different conventions they notice. When they are done, two students from each group of four should find two students from a different group of four to create a new group. Then each partnership in the new group should explain their list to the other group members. Their explanation should include where they found each convention and how they know it is that convention. They may use the Poetry Conventions anchor chart as support.

Share:

Each new group of four will share the poetry conventions it identified. The teacher should discuss any conventions misunderstood or not identified by the students.

Assess:

Notice students who need further intervention.

Further Steps:

- Give each student a poem to read in the bathroom line. The children can talk quietly about the conventions they notice in their poem while waiting for their turn.
- Ask students to read both poetry and prose during independent reading time in the reading workshop. At share, ask the students to describe what is the same and what is different in poetry and prose.

• • •   TEST TALK LESSON

STRATEGY

Identify poetry test talk and understand its meaning

Target Question:

Can I find and understand poetry test talk?

Materials:

- Poetry Test Talk anchor chart
- Practice test poem and test questions transparency
- Student copies of practice poem

Demonstration:

The teacher reminds students that yesterday they started reviewing poetry conventions. Today they will practice identifying poetry test talk and determining its meaning. She asks, "What words, phrases, and questions might you notice in poetry test talk?" Students might suggest answers such as *stanza*, *line*, *speaker of the poem*, etc. Next, the teacher leads a shared reading of the practice poem and test questions. She demonstrates slow, careful reading and rereading of the directions, test poem, questions, and answer choices. As she reads the questions, she circles the test talk and models her thinking about the meaning of the test talk included in each question. She also models any test-taking strategies she deems important. She gives the students time to observe, discuss, and question. The teacher refers to the established Test Talk anchor chart for support.

Student Practice: Numbered Heads Together Game

The teacher explains that the students will identify poetry test talk by playing a game called Numbered Heads Together. The teacher divides the class into two teams and gives each child a number so that each team has a person that is a one, a two, etc. Then the teacher places another practice poem and question on the overhead projector. She reads it with the children and says, "Numbered heads together." The teams huddle together and talk about the test talk in the question and what it means. Everyone in the group must help because anyone could be called on. When time is up, the teacher calls out a number, like four, and the students from each team with the number four come to the front of the room and describe the test talk and its meaning in the given question. The teacher could continue the game with test questions on the overhead projector or hand out a packet of poems and questions to the students.

Share:

Ask students to talk to a buddy about something new they noticed about poetry test talk. When the buddy talk is through, each partnership should share out to the whole group.

Assess:

Notice students who need further intervention.

PRACTICE WITH TEXT LESSON   • • •

Target Question:

Can I apply my knowledge of content, poetry test talk, and test-taking strategies to answer multiple-choice questions about poetry?

Materials:
- "Grandma" transparency
- "Poetry Stands" transparency
- "Poetry Stands" student copy
- Poetry Conventions anchor chart

STRATEGY

Synthesizing content, test talk, and test-taking strategy knowledge

- Test Talk anchor chart
- Test-Taking Strategies anchor chart

Demonstration:

The teacher tells students that today is the big day. Today they will use their knowledge of poetry, test talk, and test-taking strategies to practice answering poetry questions. She places the Poetry Conventions anchor chart, Poetry Test Talk anchor chart, and Test-Taking Strategies anchor chart in full view. The teacher asks students to turn to a buddy and talk about the following questions, one at a time:

What do you know about poetry and its conventions?
What test talk do you know for poetry questions?
What strategies might you use when answering these questions?

After discussing each question, the students share their thoughts.

The teacher puts the transparency of "Grandma" and the questions about it on the overhead.

DEMONSTRATION POEM:

From *A Writing Kind of Day: Poems for Young Poets* (Fletcher 2005, 10)

Directions: Read the poem and answer the questions that follow.

Grandma

1   My Grandma loves to cook Italian:
2   manicotti, veal cutlet parmesan,
3   crusty bread like you've never had.

4   Over the years she's cut so much garlic
5   the smell is soaked forever
6   into her warped cutting board.

7   Now she's losing her memory.
8   But she still remembers
9   the summer I was three.

10 "You loved to play with the garden hose

11 but you kept turning around to say:

12 DON'T SHUT IT OFF, GRANDMA!"

13 She nods off while we're talking,

14 the skin on her hands so white

15 it could almost be made from clouds.

16 I slide a pillow behind her head,

17 wrap the old blue blanket around her,

18 whisper: Don't shut it off, Grandma.

1. In the fifth stanza, the poem's words give the feeling of

A reflection.

B joy.

C guilt.

D love.

2. Which line tells of Grandma falling asleep during conversation?

A 9

B 11

C 14

D 13

The teacher leads a shared reading of "Grandma." They read the poem twice and then read the questions. The teacher begins the poem again and thinks aloud about her strategy use. "The first thing I need to do is read the directions and underline the verbs. I need to *read* and *answer*. Now I need to read the poem again. I notice that the test author put numbers on each line of the poem. I wonder if there will be a question referring to a particular line?"

Then she reads the questions. "I know I understand lots of things about poetry, but can I understand a poetry test question?" Next the teacher discusses the meaning of the test talk in each question. "Well, this question is about the sixth stanza, so I need to look at the poem and the white space and count down to the sixth stanza. That's the one that begins with 'I slide a pillow...' Then it says, '...poem's words give the feeling of....' Hmmm....I think that means how the words in that stanza make you feel, like sad or mad." The teacher continues to model understanding of test talk and knowledge of content to answer the questions. As she continues to think aloud, she also discusses her use of test-taking strategies. "Let me read the answer choices again. Well, I know it isn't... because....The answer couldn't be...because.... I have eliminated two stupid answers. Now I just need to choose from the two answers that are left." Having thoroughly modeled her thinking process with the demonstration poem and two questions provided, the students should be ready to work independently.

Student Practice:

The teacher hands out the following practice sheet to individual students, partners, or small groups. She explains that it is their turn to use all their smarts to answer some practice test questions. She asks them to repeat the process modeled for them in the demonstration. After they complete the practice sheet, they should be able to explain the test talk in the questions and what it meant, and describe the strategies they used to answer the questions and the thinking that led to their answers. She suggests that they make notes in the margins so they can remember which particular strategies they used.

STUDENT PRACTICE POEM:

From: *A Writing Kind of Day: Poems for Young Poets* (Fletcher 2005, 28)

Directions: Read the poem and answer the questions that follow.

Poetry Stands

1   They wanted to level
2   our favorite forest.

3   Our class sent the mayor
4   a swarm of angry verse;

5   we pelted the newspaper
6   with a blizzard of poems.

7   At my cousin's funeral
8   her family stood up
9   armed with nothing
10 but tears and poetry.

11 Poetry must wound
12 or heal those wounds.

13 When everyone else sits,
14 Poetry stands.

1. Which of the following is a theme of the poem?

   A friendship
   B power of poetry
   C poetry heals wounds
   D grief

2. In the third stanza, the words "armed with nothing but tears and poetry" suggest that

   A poems can make you cry.
   B the family was sad.
   C the family cried and read poetry at the funeral.
   D the cousin loved poetry.

3. In lines thirteen and fourteen, the speaker suggests that

   A poetry is influential.
   B people sit down to read poetry.
   C poetry is a good friend.
   D everyone enjoys poetry.

STUDENT PRACTICE POEM:

From: *Am I Naturally This Crazy?* (Holbrook 1996, 38)

Directions: Read the poem and answer the questions that follow.

Losing My Senses

My smeller is stopped,
it hurts when I speak.
I'm cold in the toes
and hot in the cheek.

I couldn't taste chili peppers,
I am plugged but I drain.
My ears are all jammed
and my head's a big pain.

I'm losing my senses
one by one
ever since my poor nose
went red-on-the-run.

1. The speaker is complaining of

    A a broken nose.
    B chicken pox.
    C a cold.
    D a stomachache.

2. What is the rhyme pattern used in the poem "Losing My Senses"?

    A abba
    B abab
    C aabb
    D abcb

Share:

The teacher places the practice poems and questions on the overhead so that the students can talk from them as they share. Students should explain the test talk in the questions and what it means, strategies they used to answer, and the thinking that led to their answers.

Assess:
The teacher takes note of students who need further intervention.

Further Steps:
Ask another class taking the test to buddy up with your class. Buddies could use sample poems to teach each other what they know about the conventions of poetry. Then the partnerships could create test questions together and test other partners.

"Emma Kate is the elephant; she is telling the story!" Jen Orr proclaims as she stands holding the book, *Emma Kate*, by Patricia Polacco (2005). Jennifer Kalletta jumps in. "I can't really make up my mind. Sometimes I think the book is being told from the elephant's point of view and sometimes from the girl's," she says.

It is three o'clock, students have left the building, and teachers are beginning to gather in hallways and classrooms for a little chitchat with their colleagues before they start preparing for the next school day. Jen and Jennifer, both upper-grade teachers at Annandale Terrace, are involved in a passionate conversation.

"Patricia Polacco drops tons of clues into the illustrations that the elephant is real," Jennifer says. "Look, the thermometer in the elephant's mouth and the pencil in the elephant's trunk are in color."

"Also, the license plate says *Big Mome*, which implies that the driver is an elephant, so the elephant must be real," Jen adds. "In that same picture, the car tires are flat on the elephant's side, which means that that side is carrying real extra weight."

"But the material in the girl's dress is the same material in the bedspread, which might mean the girl is dreaming about the elephant and that part of her outfit is in the dream," says Jennifer.

"It could be the exact opposite," says Jen. "This is my favorite clue that the story is told from the elephant's point of view and that the girl is his imaginary friend." On the page where the girl and the elephant are in a hospital bed, she points to the medical chart. Under the name Emma Kate is the word *pachyderm*. Jen smiles, feeling victorious.

Just then, Pat Altenburger, a fourth-grade teacher at Annandale Terrace, walks in and listens for a moment. "This is easy to settle," she says. "If you read the inside flap it says there is a twist at the end. Until the very end, Patricia Polacco leads us to believe that Emma Kate is the girl and that the elephant is her imaginary friend, but it is really the other way around. She tells us there is going to be a twist, and that is the twist. Besides, look at the end where the elephant is being tucked in by the elephant parents."

"But Pat, the flap isn't written by the author," says Jen. "Somebody from the publishing company decided what to write on the flap, not Patricia Polacco." Jennifer changes the direction of the conversation. "I was thinking that in the movie *The Wizard of Oz*, Dorothy's real life is in black and white and her whole dream about Oz is in color."

The snippet of conversation between Jen, Jennifer, and Pat shows the need for readers to use not only background knowledge but also the text and illustrations to comprehend text. As readers and test takers, students must understand that inferring is not just an opinion based on their own life experience; it is grounded in text. Cris Tovani (2000) says, "When readers infer, they need a healthy dose of textual evidence combined with a moderate measure of background knowledge" (103). Learning this important skill allows readers to read between the lines and understand what the author hasn't written. It also lets them experience success on the numerous inference questions that appear on standardized tests.

"To infer, in a pure sense, is to build meaning," wrote Ellin Oliver Keene and Susan Zimmerman in *Mosaic of Thought* (1997, 161). Readers need to infer to gain full meaning from text. Inferring is a sophisticated intellectual process but can be explained by suggesting that an inference occurs at the junction of a reader's background knowledge *and* what is stated in the text or pictured in the illustrations. Authors leave clues, like footprints, across a text or illustrations, and readers must identify the clues and then interpret them using their own experiences and individual knowledge of the world. At the end of this sophisticated mental process lies a new version of the reader's thinking, which will continue to grow and change. As in the conversation above, inferences can become more thoughtful when people have the opportunity to discuss, compare, and merge their thoughts.

As teachers, we don't usually give students a set of questions to answer after they read a text; we want their reading experiences in school to mirror what real readers do. Instead we offer many opportunities to discuss reading, as we would with our friends and family. Coupled with discussion, writing about the thinking that occurs during reading can also be an effective tool for deepening understanding. Yet standardized tests require the ability to read a passage (prose or poetry), read the questions that follow, reread the passage to determine whether a question is explicit or implicit, and then answer the questions using the necessary mental processes. All of this must be accomplished without the benefit of discussion or even much time to think.

So how do we ready students for these questions without denying them opportunities for authentic reading and discussion? Teaching students the mental processes involved in inferring is essential. All students need demonstrations of the steps required to accomplish different kinds of thinking in relation to test questions. If they understand the process needed for reading and thinking, they are much more likely to use that process as test takers.

Pat Altenburger models that process for her fourth-grade students. She wants them to be aware that dialogue between characters is chock full of clues that help readers understand characters and their traits. It is not the first or second lesson in the unit, but it is early. She doesn't want her students to overlook dialogue in their quest for meaning.

Before this lesson or series of lessons, she has taught the students that inferring is grounded in their background knowledge *and* the text and illustrations. Inferring has also been part of many other lessons and units. She understands that her students are in different stages of this learning, and she expects this lesson to be another opportunity to practice, with her support. As they become accustomed to her request for evidence from the text to support their inferences, students are beginning to internalize this important part of the mental process.

Beginning a Unit About Inferring

Readers use dialogue to help themselves infer characters traits. Pat Altenburger writes this sentence on the whiteboard as her students approach the carpet and ready themselves for reading workshop. She turns to her students, checks their body language, reminds one child to turn toward the easel, and then reads her mini-lesson statement. Then she reads it again.

"Today we are going to look closely at the dialogue in one of our favorites, *Freedom Summer* (2001) by Deborah Wiles, and see how it helps us get to know the characters better," Pat says. "We will need to make inferences, as the author doesn't just tell us about each character. Can someone remind us what our brain does in order to use this 'mind tool'?"

Nicholas says, "We have to use what the author wrote in the text to infer. We also have to use our schema. We have to combine our schema with what the text says."

"Thanks, Nicholas. Just a reminder that the text can include the illustrations," says Pat. She leans toward the easel and writes *schema + text = inference* on the board. "Don't forget what we talked about on Monday. It's like a math problem, *a + b = c*. It is not an inference if you don't gather information from *(a)* your schema and *(b)* the text and/or illustrations. There is no *c*, an inference, unless you use *a* and *b*." Then she asks them to talk to a knee buddy about what they are thinking.

Yeimi and Marisa start to chat right away. Marisa says, "When I infer, the first thing I do is use my schema, but I know that that doesn't really help me. I have to pay attention to what the author writes, too." Pat listens in and takes some notes on her clipboard. In another minute, she asks the kids to turn back to her. They share their comments, and Pat takes a few more notes.

From the conversations, Pat knows that after several days of focusing on inferring, most of her students are really catching on to what is required to make a strong inference. She knows how important it is as a reader and thinker (and as a person) to be able to "read between the lines," and she also knows that many questions on the SOL reading test require the ability to infer. Because she has read through released items, she knows the test is likely to include questions about characters, so she needs to include this subject in her unit on inferring.

Because her students love stories about her life and her children, Pat tells a quick personal anecdote in order to draw them in. "Recently, Max and Leah's young cousins visited from New Jersey. Now, you know Max and Leah are teenagers and like to be with their friends, play on the computer, and talk on the phone. Well, I was telling them about the visit and expected that they would complain about having to spend time with the little girls instead of their friends. Then Max said, 'Let's take them to the pool during their visit.' I was stunned. Max hadn't wanted to go to the pool all summer!"

Then Pat wrote on the easel, *Max is kind and can be selfless*. "I know this because he suggested the swimming pool for his little cousins even though I know he didn't really want to go. He knew that they would like it, and he was willing to go for them. When he said just that one little thing, I could tell so much about who he really is. I used what Max said and my schema about Max to make an inference about his character, just like we are going to do with *Freedom Summer*.

"Next, let's look at some dialogue between Joe and John Henry in *Freedom Summer*. If we infer, this dialogue should be able to tell us quite a bit about the boys." The children have already heard this powerful text many times, so Pat is free to use just a piece of it with the understanding that the students already know the whole story. It would be atypical for Pat to use a part of text in a mini-lesson if the class had not read and discussed the story at least once.

Pat tapes a four-column chart on the easel with the columns labeled Character Name, Dialogue, Character Trait Inference, and Evidence from Text. She places a transparency of a page from the text in which John Henry and Joe are sitting on the diving board. (The book has no page numbers.) She reads the page twice. Then she underlines the part where John Henry says, "White folks don't want colored folks in their pool." Pat says, "Hmmm...I notice that right above this dialogue, the author tells us that John Henry's voice shakes. That is information that will help me infer. I know that when Leah and Max are really upset with each other, Max's voice can sound funny, kind of like it's quivering. It's because he is mad and upset and trying to control his emotions. So I am inferring that John Henry feels angry and upset because he understands that some of the white people in the town don't want to swim in the same pool with the black people. I think John Henry is insightful; he understands the reason why the pool is being filled with tar."

She moves to the chart and records John Henry's name in the first column, the dialogue in the second column, and the word *insightful* in the third column. In the last column she writes, "White folks don't want colored folks in their pool" again. In this case, it is the dialogue that is the evidence from the text. Pat feels the chart is an important part of her modeling. She wants the students to hear *and* see her very active thinking process. This will help them repeat the process in their own reading and on the test.

Although Pat is teaching a unit on inferring in reading workshop, the idea of inferring has already been integrated into other units such as main idea, author's intent, and visualizing. In addition, the process was taught during word study, vocabulary lessons, poetry workshop, and lessons with the school counselor in reading body language. The class has been keeping an Inferring anchor chart since the first month of school. The chart now contains words like *theme, moral, unknown words,* and *body language.* Each time the students are exposed to concepts that require inferring, that concept is recorded on the chart. As Pat finishes filling out the four-column chart, she turns and writes the words *character traits using dialogue* on the anchor chart, then reads it aloud. "This is another kind of inferring we do as readers and test takers," she says.

She starts again. "I also infer that John Henry is grown-up for his age. He and his friend are so disappointed about the swimming pool, yet he isn't throwing a temper tantrum the way some kids might. He is just talking to his friend about what he thinks. This makes me think of some more character traits. I think John Henry is not afraid to share how he feels. He is forthright and honest." She records her comments on the four-column chart.

Pat stops talking for a few seconds and lets what she has said and written sink in. Then she says, "Please talk to your knee buddy about what I just said." Kate and Isabel can't help talking about their own feelings about what is happening in the book.

Isabel says, "It's not fair that they can't go to the same swimming pool. I can't believe the town filled the pool in so no one can swim." Pat listens to many of the reactions around the room. Even though her students have heard this book before, they still get caught up the unfairness of what has happened. She stops their talk and clarifies her instructions; she realizes that her first set of directions might have been too general.

"Boys and girls," Pat says, "I would like you to talk to your knee buddy again, but this time I want you to talk about how I supported my inferences about John Henry's character traits."

Raymond and Ki Won jump back into conversation. Raymond says, "I think Ms. Altenburger thinks John Henry acts grown-up because she knows that when some people are really disappointed or upset, they throw a tantrum, and the book says his voice was only shaky."

"Yeah, Ms. Altenburger used her schema about people," says Ki Won. Pat notes that Ki Won noticed only the background knowledge piece of her inference. Later in the week, she plans to teach some small-group lessons to kids who need extra support with inferring, and she will be sure to include Ki Won.

The students finish their conversations and share. Pat underlines another piece of dialogue, from Joe, John Henry's best friend. "'You're wrong, John Henry,' I say, but I know he's right."

"Please talk to a knee buddy about what Joe said and about what you can infer about Joe's character traits from the dialogue. Be ready to prove your inference with evidence from the text and your schema. Remember: $a + b = c$." After the students talk, Pat calls on Priya. "What do you notice about the kind of person Joe is, Priya? Remember I said that I inferred that John Henry is mature, insightful, and honest."

Priya says, "I think he is empathetic." (That word comes straight from the counselor's last lesson.)

"Why?" asks Pat.

Priya answers, "Right after Joe says that John Henry is wrong, he says to himself that he knows he is right. He kind of understands how his friend is feeling and he is trying to protect him." Pat turns back to the four-column chart and records Priya's thoughts about Joe.

The class spends the next day rereading and thinking some more about the dialogue in *Freedom Summer* and how it informs their thoughts about John Henry and Joe. As the students become more fluent with the skill, Pat adds more character traits to the four-column chart, always careful to ask for the evidence from the text that supports the inference. She also rereads the Inferring anchor chart and reiterates that character traits are one kind of inferring question that will appear on the test. On the third day, she gives each student a page of *Freedom Summer* and a personal copy of the four-column chart. She asks them to find one piece of dialogue, infer one character trait, and record it on the chart.

Wrapping It Up: Test Talk Lesson

As Pat finishes teaching the unit on inferring she considers what will be important to teach her students about the test talk on the subject. Countless questions on standardized tests require inference, including questions on the many topics addressed in previous chapters of this book. She studies the released items and then creates a practice packet with two passages and five questions following each. She wants the students to be able not only to recognize questions that require an inference, but also to identify the language in those questions that suggests the need to infer. This lesson is not about answering the question, but about recognizing them.

The students come in from recess, settle in, and come to the gather space. The class Inferring anchor chart is on the easel. This anchor chart is a list of the kinds of thinking that readers do that require inferring: understanding character traits, predicting, visualizing, comparing, theme, moral, and author's intent. Pat wants the chart to support the students on their journey to locate test talk.

"Today we are going to read some test questions and decide if they are questions that require us to infer, or if the answer is just in the text. As we discussed before, it's like knowing if the author answered the question for you or if you have to use your schema. I want to remind you how important rereading the passage is going to be." Pat writes *reread* on the easel. "If you reread, you will be able to tell if the answer is right in the text, or if you'll have to use your schema to help answer the question. If you don't reread, your answer will not be the smartest it can be."

Pat asks the children to form groups of four, then gives each group a packet. She tells them she wants them to read the packet together and decide which questions require inferring and which don't. She asks them to mark the inferring questions with highlighters. The students find a group space around the room and get to work. Pat approaches a group and listens in. Marisa says, "After I reread the first question under the passage about trains, I reread the passage. The answer is right in the second paragraph. Ms. Altenburger said that there would be some questions where the author would just tell us that answer. That's what number 1 is."

Pat moves on to another group. Raymond says, "It says 'One idea presented in both of these selections is . . . .' First, I think *selections* are like passages, which is the text we have to read. I think we have to reread both of these passages and find some themes and see if any of them are the same. The second passage has a question about both of the selections. We have to compare the two passages. I think that is what the test author means by *idea*. This is definitely an inference question."

Pat says, "Oh, Raymond, that was really smart to use the clues in the question and what you know about tests to understand that *selection* means *passage*. Good thinking."

In about fifteen minutes, Pat asks the class to return to share. The kids come up and sit facing the Inferring anchor chart. Pat has placed a blank chart entitled Inferring Test Talk next to the anchor chart. "OK," Pat says, "let's get started. Did anyone find a question that is not answered by the author directly in the text? These are questions where you will have to find the answer by using the text plus your schema."

Raymond raises his hand. Pat knows he is going to share the compare question. This will be a hard one for the class to get started with. Raymond says, "My group found one. It is after the second passage. It says, 'One idea presented in both of these selections is . . . .' You have to compare."

"What specific language in that question makes you think it is an inference question?" asks Pat.

"Well, the word *idea* I think is like theme, and *presented* is like what the authors are telling us," says Raymond.

"What should I put on our Test Talk chart, Raymond?" asks Pat.

"I think you should put 'One idea presented in both of these selections is...' but then underline *idea* and *presented* because those are the clue words."

"Terrific," says Pat. "Let's follow Raymond's lead. Be prepared to tell me your test talk question or phrase but also the clue words. Who else has test talk to share?"

Priya raises her hand. "My group found this question, 'What does the author suggest by stating . . . ?' We think it is an inference question because that word *suggest* is like *hint*. That means the author doesn't just give us the answer. We have to infer."

"Did you reread to make sure the author doesn't answer?"

"Yes," says Priya.

"So you think a clue word should be *suggest*?" asks Pat.

Priya nods and says, "You should write, 'What does the author suggest by stating . . .' and underline *suggest*."

"Priya, what about the word *stating*? Do you know what that means?"

Priya shakes her head, and Destiny jumps in. "I think it is like what the author writes or says," says Destiny.

"Yes, so the question is asking you to be able to infer what the author means by stating or telling us something. So, I'll underline *stating* too. That will remind us that we have to reread what the author states."

Seung Hee waits until Pat writes on the chart and then raises her hand. She says, "We found another one. Question 8 says, 'In paragraph 3, the word...means....'"

"Tell me about that one, Seung Hee," says Pat.

"I think there will be lots of questions like this one," the girl replies. "Test authors always want to know what a word means."

Pat smiled and asked, "Why is this an inferring question?"

Seung Hee says, "Well, you have to use the words around the unknown word and your schema to figure out the hard word."

"OK, what should I write on the chart, Seung Hee?"

"I think you should write, 'The word...means....' and underline *means*. *Means* is the clue word. That's like what does it mean or what is the meaning of that word."

Pat asks for two more examples of inference questions and clue words and adds them to the Inferring Test Talk chart. She doesn't want to overwhelm the students. Inference questions are a broad topic, and there is quite a bit of language to think about. She doesn't expect them to memorize every possible clue word; she just wants to give them a taste of what words might be a strong signal that they need to infer. She plans to do one more day of charting language, and then she wants them to compare the language they have charted with language that might signal a literal question. Pat thinks her students will notice a strong difference in the language of the two types of questions, and that difference will inform their thinking on test day.

Reading test questions to decide whether they are implicit—and require inferring—or explicit is *very careful, very active* reading. We have to prepare students for this level of intellectual rigor, beginning in kindergarten, by teaching them that reading is thinking.

CONCEPT REVIEW LESSON   • • •

Target Question:
Do I remember how to make an inference?

Materials:
• Cold weather clothes (hat, gloves, heavy coat, boots, blanket)

STRATEGY

Inferring information from a text

- Set of keys
- Practice passages and questions
- Chart paper

Demonstration:

The teacher dresses up in cold weather clothes, holds her keys, and reads the following message and questions, already written on the board.

I am going on vacation.
What am I wearing on my head?
What kind of shoes am I wearing?
To what kind of climate do you think I am traveling?
What transportation do you think I'm using?

The teacher reviews the questions one at a time. The students discuss the probable answers to each question. Next, the teacher points out that the first two questions can be answered simply by looking at her clothes and *observing* the information. However, the third and fourth questions require different thinking, called making *inferences*. The teacher asks the students why they thought that she was driving to a cold climate when she did not tell or show them where or how she was traveling. The students will say they noticed her clothes and keys. The teacher explains that they are now combining what they observe with their schema to draw a conclusion or make a guess about what is probably true. They are observing and thinking, which is the definition of *inferring*. She tells them that like the observing and thinking they did in this exercise, they can read and think to make inferences from text. She reminds them of the equation they learned for generating a response to a question when the answer is not directly in the text: Text + Schema = Inference, or $a + b = c$.

The teacher reminds the students that the reading test will contain passages and questions about the passages. Sometimes the students will be able to find the answers right in the text, but sometimes they will have to *infer* the answers. During their inferring unit of study, as well as other units like main idea, they learned that good readers use inferring for many different reasons, including defining unknown words, finding main ideas or themes, making predictions, identifying character's feelings and traits, and creating personal interpretations. The teacher discusses each type of inference and offers examples of when each type might be used.

Student Practice:

The teacher groups students and gives one of the following passages to each group. Each group is to read its passage, decide which inference type is required, and generate an appropriate inference using their schema and the text. The teacher reminds students that when readers infer, they should use their schema and experience, but they also must use the textual clues. In other words, the students must be able to defend their inferences by using the text. Each group member will be required to discuss part of the group's thinking process during share time.

PRACTICE PASSAGES:

1. We could not believe that Dave forgot to wear pants to school! When he opened the door and stood there in his underwear, we were *dumbfounded*!

What does the word *dumbfounded* mean?

2. Sara was always forgetting her homework. Her parents had lectured her over and over again about it, but she'd done it again. Here it was, Friday afternoon, and she had to take *another* note home from her teacher saying that she had missed recess because she forgot her homework.

How did Sara probably feel as she walked home on Friday?

3. Paul ate pizza every day. He ate pizza for breakfast, lunch, and dinner.

What type of pizza does the author suggest is Paul's favorite?

Share:

The students gather, and the teacher puts each passage and question one at a time on the overhead. Groups discuss what type of inference was required (unknown word, feelings, or prediction) as well as the text and schema that they used to create the inference and answer each question.

Assess:

During practice and share, the teacher circulates and notes which students need small-group intervention to strengthen this skill.

Further Steps:

- Practice making different types of inferences during class meetings or activity time.

  You might have students consider questions like these:

1. What can you infer about how someone is feeling by their body language? Facial expressions? Behavior?
2. What would a visitor infer about your class by observing what is hanging on the walls?
3. What would a friend infer about you by a quick peek into your bedroom?
4. What does your teacher infer when you don't do your homework? What about when you work really hard on a project?

● ● ●   TEST TALK LESSON

<table>
<tr><td>

STRATEGY

Identifying inferring test talk

</td><td>

Target Question:

Can I find and understand inferring test talk?

Materials:

- Inferring Test Talk anchor chart from inferring unit of study completed previously in Reading Workshop
- Overhead of sample test passage with accompanying inferring questions
- Chart paper
- Sticky notes

Demonstration:

The teacher begins by reminding students that some questions on their reading test will require them to find answers that they won't be able to

</td></tr>
</table>

"put their finger on" in the accompanying text, because the information needed is not explicitly written. When this exciting challenge arises on the test, students will use the text and their schema to help create the answer, or make an inference. The teacher reminds the students that asking themselves the following question will help them know when to infer: "Does the author answer this question for me in the text, or do I have to help?" The teacher explains that identifying test talk also helps test takers know what type of skill a question is asking them to use. In order to show their inferring knowledge on the reading test, they will first have to identify the inferring questions by translating tricky test talk. Their objective today is to remember the test talk that signals that they are being asked to infer.

The teacher reads the demonstration passage and multiple-choice questions on the overhead and asks the students to use the Inferring anchor chart to help her identify and circle the test talk that is particular to inferring. Examples might include "the author suggests," "the reader can tell," "the character feels," etc.

Next she underlines the verbs in the directions that help her know what to do with the question. Finally, she asks what test-taking strategies might best be used as tools to help answer inferring questions. Possibilities may include active reading, rereading, and activating schema.

Student Practice: Test Talk Trivia Game

The teacher tells the class that since today is the last test talk lesson, they will review all the test talk they've learned to prepare them to tackle the test. She divides the class into five teams (or as many as units reviewed) and assigns each team a test talk category. For example, Team One might be main idea while Team Two is author's intent. Teams are given sticky notes and told to write at least five test questions (one question per sticky note) in their category, using the corresponding anchor chart as a resource. Every team member must contribute at least one question, and every question must contain subject-specific test talk.

Share:

The teacher collects all sticky notes and asks students to gather with their teams at the front of the room. She puts a columned chart on the board, with a unit title as each column's heading. She reads the students' sample test questions one at a time, and the teams are to decide together in which column to place each question. At the end of the share time, the completed chart encapsulates the students' learning about test talk for the whole year. The teacher and students discuss different ways that their test talk knowledge will help them on the test, recording their ideas at the bottom of the chart. Ideas might include using the test talk to help them decide what reading schema to activate for each question.

Assess:

During practice and share time, the teacher takes note of students who are still not able to identify test talk. She finds time to reteach during small group or individual conferences before the test.

• • •   PRACTICE WITH TEXTS LESSON

STRATEGY

Synthesizing content, test talk, and test-taking knowledge

Target Question:

Can I use my knowledge of inferring, inferring test talk, and test-taking strategies to answer multiple-choice questions?

Materials:

- Transparency of demonstration page and accompanying questions
- Several copies each of student practice passage and inferring multiple-choice questions (The practice passage and questions should be teacher-generated to ensure that format and language mirror your test as closely as possible.)
- Transparencies of student practice passage and questions

Demonstration:

The teacher tells students that today they will put their knowledge about inferring, inferring test talk, and test-taking strategies "to the test!" Before they begin, she will lead a think-aloud to demonstrate how a smart test taker attacks an inferring question. She puts the Inferring Test Talk anchor chart and the Test-Taking Strategies chart on the board to use as references.

The teacher puts a transparency of the demonstration page on the overhead.

Use the following passage to answer numbers 4, 5, and 6.

Tara was eight years old, and she still didn't know how to swim. She avoided the pool, staying away because she didn't want her friends to discover how afraid she was of the water. One afternoon, her mother told her that there was a letter for her in the mail! Tara was very excited until she ripped open the envelope and read the words on the front: "YOU'RE INVIT-ED TO A POOL PARTY!" Her eyes filled with tears and her hand shook as she dropped the invitation on the floor. She didn't want to miss the party, so she knew she was going to have to find a way to learn how to swim!

4. In line two, what does *avoided* mean?

   A loved
   B stayed away
   C thought about
   D watched

5. When Tara saw that the letter was an invitation to a pool party, she felt

   A excited.
   B afraid.
   C angry.
   D tired.

6. In line eight, what does the author suggest that Tara will do next?

   A throw the card away and try to forget about the party
   B tell all of her friends she can't swim
   C ask someone to teach her how to swim
   D plan a bowling party so she won't have to swim

The teacher begins a think-aloud that might sound like this: "The first thing I notice about this test page is the directions. I know that I should always read directions carefully, so I'll do that first. I'm going to underline the word *use* because that will help me remember that I'll be using this text to answer the next three questions. I think I'll read the passage once first and then check out the questions so I know what I'm looking for when I reread and know what reading schema I'll need to activate."

The teacher reads the passage and the question. "The question says, 'The word *avoided* means....' Hmmm...I remember that questions about words I don't know require me to use the context to make an *unknown word inference*. I'm going to go back to line one and look for context that might help me define *avoided*. I see that after the word *avoided* it says *stayed away*. That makes sense to me! Someone who doesn't know how to swim would certainly want to stay away from the pool. See how I'm using the text *and* my schema about swimming to answer this question? Remember our equation? Text + Schema = Inference, or $a + b = c$. Look, *stayed away* is an answer choice, and I know these other choices don't make sense, so I can eliminate them. I think I've got the best answer.

"Let's go to number 5. This one asks me how Tara felt when she got the invitation. Since *felt* is an inference test talk word, I'm going to circle that to remind myself that I'm making a *feelings inference*. Well, I know how I'd feel if I got an invitation to a pool party...so excited! But I know that I can't only use my own schema to infer; I have to use the text, too. I'm going to reread the part when Tara got the invitation so I can make a good inference. The text says that after she read the card, 'Her eyes filled with tears and her hand shook as she dropped the invitation on the floor.' My schema tells me that this isn't the way someone who is excited acts. I'm going to start eliminating choices until I find a feeling that matches how Tara acted." The teacher models elimination until the best answer is chosen.

The teacher models the process again to answer number 6, emphasizing test talk, strategy use, and use of the text and schema to make a prediction inference.

Student Practice:

The teacher tells the students that it's their turn to practice. She asks students to partner up and passes out practice passage and questions. Students work together to identify the inferring test talk, decide what type of inferring each question will require, and answer the questions. The teacher reminds the students that they will be asked to share the text and schema they used to answer each question.

Share:

The teacher shows the practice passage on the overhead and each group discusses the process it used to find the answers. Students tell how they identified the test talk and type of inference required, and share the text and schema they used to make their inference. Finally, students share the test-taking strategies they used to isolate the best answer.

Assess:

For students who are still struggling with the concept of making inferences, the teacher makes time for small-group work with other sample texts.

Further Steps:

Using sample texts, practice making other types of inferences not addressed in this lesson, like identifying themes and morals. Create an inferring literacy activity for students to access during reading workshop, rotating activities that encourage students to practice making different types of inferences. During share times, encourage students to share inferences made during their independent reading.

Conclusion:
Embracing the Testing Challenge

It's the afternoon before the SOL test in Jen Orr's fifth-grade class, and the students are gathered at Jen's feet. Jen reads Dr. Seuss's *Hooray for Diffendooffer Day!* (1998) then rereads this page:

Miss Bonkers rose. "Don't fret!" she said.
"You've learned the things you need
To pass that test and many more—
I'm certain you'll succeed.
We've taught you that the earth is round,
That red and white make pink,
And something else that matters more—
We've taught you how to think."

After she finishes reading, Jen asks the students if the Dr. Seuss story helps them feel ready for tomorrow's test. Fredy says, "That story is just like us. They have worked really hard like us, and they are ready like we are. The test is going to be easy!"

Jen says, "Isn't it interesting how challenges feel exciting and easy when you are ready for them? Can anybody tell me why the test will be easy?"

Silbia raises her hand excitedly and says, "It's going to be easy because we understand it. We know test talk and we know lots of reading strategies to use."

Sindi adds, "Ms. Orr, that book and the test makes me think of my soccer team. At the beginning of our season, I used to cry before games because I didn't know the rules or how to play. That's how I felt about the SOL test last year, too. I cried before I came to school. But this year it feels different. I'm not scared because I know what it's going to be like and I know what the words mean. I also know what to do if I get stuck. I feel excited instead of scared."

We didn't feel scared anymore either. At some point during our school's ongoing journey, we stopped viewing the SOL test as an obstacle we had to help our students survive, and started seeing it as an exciting challenge we could teach our students to conquer. We realized that for years, teaching students to take tests was an invisible curriculum. We had no plans or resources to help us teach test taking in a meaningful way, nor did we have any type of mandate from the district or state to teach it as a skill. Nevertheless our ignoring this invisible curriculum left students as vulnerable as if we had neglected to teach them to write or subtract. So we did what teachers do across the country every day: we identified a teaching challenge, worked together to put some preconceived notions behind us, and used what we knew about children as learners to create a new approach to teaching test taking that worked. Our scores started rising, and most important, on test day, our students felt empowered and confident.

In Donald Graves's *The Energy to Teach* (2001), a teacher discusses the stress involved in preparing students for standardized tests. "I think teachers everywhere are so exhausted and teaching is taking so much energy because we are forced to compromise our beliefs too often" (80). We hope that the ideas in this book not only reenergize you, but revitalize your approach to test preparation without compromising *your* beliefs about how children learn.

References

Anderson, Carl. 2000. *How's It Going? A Practical Guide to Conferring with Student Writers*. Portsmouth, NH: Heinemann.

Bishop, Rudine, ed. 1999. *The Best Children's Poems of Effie Lee Newsome*. Honesdale, PA: Boyds Mills.

Calkins, Lucy, Kate Montgomery, Donna Santman, and Beverly Falk. 1998. *A Teacher's Guide to Standardized Reading Tests: Knowledge Is Power*. Portsmouth, NH: Heinemann.

Dead Poets Society. 1989. DVD. Directed by Peter Weir. Burbank, CA: Touchstone Studios.

Dr. Seuss, and Jack Prelutsky. 1998. *Hooray for Diffendoofer Day!* New York: Alfred A. Knopf.

Fletcher, Ralph. 2005. *A Writing Kind of Day: Poems for Young Poets*. Honesdale, PA: Boyds Mills.

Graves, Donald H. 2001. *The Energy to Teach*. Portsmouth, NH: Heinemann.

Greenfield, Eloise. 1978. *Honey, I Love and Other Poems*. New York: HarperCollins.

Grimes, Nikki. 1997. *It's Raining Laughter*. Honesdale, PA: Boyds Mills.

Harvey, Stephanie, and Anne Goudvis. 2000. *Strategies That Work: Teaching Comprehension to Enhance Understanding*. Portland, ME: Stenhouse.

Heard,Georgia. 1989. *For the Good of the Earth and Sun: Teaching Poetry*. Portsmouth, NH: Heinemann.

———. 1999. *Awakening the Heart: Exploring Poetry in Elementary and Middle School*. Portsmouth, NH: Heinemann.

Holbrook, Sara. 1996. *Am I Naturally This Crazy?* Honesdale, PA: Boyds Mills.

Hughes, Langston. 1994. *The Dream Keeper and Other Poems*. New York: Alfred A. Knopf.

Keene, Ellin Oliver, and Susan Zimmermann. 1997. *Mosaic of Thought: Teaching Comprehension in a Reader's Workshop*. Portsmouth, NH: Heinemann.

Krull, Kathleen. 1996. *Wilma Unlimited: How Wilma Rudolph Became the World's Fastest Woman*. New York: Harcourt Brace and Company.

McNaughton, Colin. 1994. *Making Friends with Frankenstein: A Book of Monstrous Poems and Pictures*. Cambridge, MA: Candlewick.

Polacco, Patricia. 1998. *Thank You, Mr. Falker*. New York: Philomel.

———. 2005. *Emma Kate*. New York: Philomel.

Prelutsky, Jack. 1994. *A Pizza the Size of the Sun*. New York: Greenwillow.

Ruurs, Margriet. 2005. *My Librarian Is a Camel: How Books Are Brought to Children Around the World*. Honesdale, PA: Boyds Mills.

Sibberson, Franki, and Karen Szymusiak. 2003. *Still Learning to Read: Teaching Students in Grades 3–6*. Portland, ME: Stenhouse.

Silverstein, Shel. 1974. *Where the Sidewalk Ends*. New York: HarperCollins.

Tovani, Cris. 2000. *I Read It, but I Don't Get It: Comprehension Strategies for Adolescent Readers*. Portland, ME: Stenhouse.

Waldman, Neil. 2003. *Dream Makers: Young People Share Their Hopes and Inspirations*. Honesdale, PA: Boyds Mills.

Weatherford, Carole. 2005. *A Negro League Scrapbook*. Honesdale, PA: Boyds Mills.

Wiles, Deborah. 2001. *Freedom Summer*. New York: Antheneum.